Christopher Hudson
with Megan Chrans

TYNDALE HOUSE PUBLISHERS, INC.

CAROL STREAM, ILLINOIS

Visit Tyndale's exciting Web site for kids at www.tyndale.com/kids.

TYNDALE is a registered trademark of Tyndale House Publishers, Inc.

Tyndale Kids logo is a trademark of Tyndale House Publishers, Inc.

JUMBLE™ and © 2010 by Tribune Media Services, Inc. All rights reserved. Used by permission.

Bible Jumble for Kids

Copyright © 2010 by Tyndale House Publishers, Inc. All rights reserved.

Cover illustration of boy and girl copyright © by Mark Stay/iStockphoto. All rights reserved.

Cover photo of chalkboard copyright © by Emrah Turudu/iStockphoto. All rights reserved.

Designed by Mark Anthony Lane II

Produced with the assistance of Hudson & Associates.

Scripture quotations are taken from the Holy Bible, New Living Translation, copyright © 1996, 2004, 2007 by Tyndale House Foundation. Used by permission of Tyndale House Publishers, Inc., Carol Stream, Illinois 60188. All rights reserved.

ISBN 978-1-4143-2696-2

Printed in the United States of America

16 15 14 13 12 11 10
7 6 5 4 3 2 1

CONTENTS

THE MAN WHO NEVER DIED

GENESIS 4:17–5:24

Unscramble the Jumbles, one letter to each space, to spell words that relate to this Scripture passage.

#1

AREH

BOX OF CLUES

STUMPED? MAYBE YOU CAN FIND A CLUE BELOW. (CLUES ARE NOT IN ORDER.)

- ~~Abel's brother~~
- Being in close community with someone
- ~~Established; discovered~~
- ~~To use your ears~~
- ~~Metal used for third-place medals~~

#2

NICA

#3

ZENBOR

#4

NOFEDUD

#5

FLIPSHOWEL

MYSTERY ANSWER:

Arrange the circled letters to solve the mystery answer.

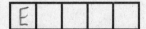

TWO BROTHERS MAKE UP
GENESIS 25:19-34; 33:1-20

Unscramble the Jumbles, one letter to each space, to spell words that relate to this Scripture passage.

#1 SUAE

BOX OF CLUES
STUMPED? MAYBE YOU CAN FIND A CLUE BELOW. (CLUES ARE NOT IN ORDER.)

- Hugged
- The hairy twin
- The twin known for being a homebody
- Not rejected
- The place Jacob settled

#2 BAJCO

#3 THUCSCO

#4 BACDREME

#5 TEECCAPD

MYSTERY ANSWER:
Arrange the circled letters to solve the mystery answer.

A STONE FOR A PILLOW
GENESIS 28:11-19

Unscramble the Jumbles, one letter to each space, to spell words that relate to this Scripture passage.

#1 REFTAH

BOX OF CLUES
STUMPED? MAYBE YOU CAN FIND A CLUE BELOW. (CLUES ARE NOT IN ORDER.)

- Many
- Set of steps
- Had a nighttime vision
- Male parent
- Opposite of taking

#2 VINGIG

#3 REEDMAD

#4 SUURMONE

#5 WRAYSITA

MYSTERY ANSWER:
Arrange the circled letters to solve the mystery answer.

3

BROTHER TROUBLE

GENESIS 37:18-30

Unscramble the Jumbles, one letter to each space, to spell words that relate to this Scripture passage.

#1 LILK

BOX OF CLUES

STUMPED? MAYBE YOU CAN FIND A CLUE BELOW. (CLUES ARE NOT IN ORDER.)

- A hole in the ground with water in it
- Someone who has nighttime visions
- To end a life
- Space between two people or places
- A big brother who wanted to rescue Joseph

#2 BEENUR

#3 MEARDER

#4 SINTREC

#5 NATCIEDS

MYSTERY ANSWER:

Arrange the circled letters to solve the mystery answer.

4

TROUBLE FOR THE EGYPTIANS

EXODUS 9–10

Unscramble the Jumbles, one letter to each space, to spell words that relate to this Scripture passage.

#1 LHIA

#2 STULCO

#3 ROOPNUDW

#4 CLOSKVITE

#5 ITLNGHGNI

BOX OF CLUES
STUMPED? MAYBE YOU CAN FIND A CLUE BELOW. (CLUES ARE NOT IN ORDER.)

- Normally accompanies thunder
- Farm animals
- Frozen balls that fall from the sky
- Grasshopper-like insect
- Heavy rainstorm

MYSTERY ANSWER:
Arrange the circled letters to solve the mystery answer.

5

THE LAST PLAGUE
EXODUS 11

Unscramble the Jumbles, one letter to each space, to spell words that relate to this Scripture passage.

#1 DLOU

BOX OF CLUES
STUMPED? MAYBE YOU CAN FIND A CLUE BELOW. (CLUES ARE NOT IN ORDER.)

- High volume
- People who live next door
- Not youngest
- People in charge
- On fire

#2 DLSETO

#3 GUNNIRB

#4 CIFFOILSA

#5 SHOEBRING

MYSTERY ANSWER:
Arrange the circled letters to solve the mystery answer.

THE BIG TEN
EXODUS 20

Unscramble the Jumbles, one letter to each space, to spell words that relate to this Scripture passage.

#1 LATES

BOX OF CLUES
STUMPED? MAYBE YOU CAN FIND A CLUE BELOW. (CLUES ARE NOT IN ORDER.)

- Come toward
- Day of rest
- What a witness might do in court
- To take what isn't yours
- Not truly

#2 ALFLYSE

#3 HABTABS

#4 TTIYSFE

#5 APAPCORH

MYSTERY ANSWER:
Arrange the circled letters to solve the mystery answer.

A HELPER FOR MOSES
EXODUS 28

Unscramble the Jumbles, one letter to each space, to spell words that relate to this Scripture passage.

#1 BORE

BOX OF CLUES
STUMPED? MAYBE YOU CAN FIND A CLUE BELOW. (CLUES ARE NOT IN ORDER.)

- A spiritual leader
- Clothing worn by a priest
- Brother of Abihu, Eleazar, and Ithamar
- Holy or set apart
- A jewel

#2 ADNAB

#3 DEARCS

#4 RESTIP

#5 STEENMOG

MYSTERY ANSWER:
Arrange the circled letters to solve the mystery answer.

8

FOOD IN THE DESERT

NUMBERS 11

Unscramble the Jumbles, one letter to each space, to spell words that relate to this Scripture passage.

#1 A T E M

BOX OF CLUES
STUMPED? MAYBE YOU CAN FIND A CLUE BELOW. (CLUES ARE NOT IN ORDER.)

- Complaining in a high-pitched voice
- Upset
- To grumble
- The meat God gave the Israelites to eat
- Beef or chicken, for example

#2 G A R Y N

#3 L U A Q I

#4 G I N W I H N

#5 L C I O N P M A

MYSTERY ANSWER:
Arrange the circled letters to solve the mystery answer.

A HERO DIES
DEUTERONOMY 34

Unscramble the Jumbles, one letter to each space, to spell words that relate to this Scripture passage.

#1 WREOP

BOX OF CLUES

STUMPED? MAYBE YOU CAN FIND A CLUE BELOW. (CLUES ARE NOT IN ORDER.)

- Made a commitment
- Mighty strength
- A person who helps his or her master
- Permitted
- How a person got to the top of a mountain

#2 ILBECDM

#3 TERVSAN

#4 WELLODA

#5 MEROPSDI

MYSTERY ANSWER:
Arrange the circled letters to solve the mystery answer.

SCOPING OUT THE CITY
JOSHUA 1–2

Unscramble the Jumbles, one letter to each space, to spell words that relate to this Scripture passage.

#1 NOSRGT

BOX OF CLUES
STUMPED? MAYBE YOU CAN FIND A CLUE BELOW. (CLUES ARE NOT IN ORDER.)

- Brave
- Dangling
- Mighty
- River that marked the eastern boundary of the land
- Where Rahab lived

#2 CRIJOHE

#3 GANHNIG

#4 PSUHAREET

#5 SUGAROUCEO

MYSTERY ANSWER:
Arrange the circled letters to solve the mystery answer.

THE DAY THE SUN AND MOON STAND STILL

JOSHUA 10:1-15

Unscramble the Jumbles, one letter to each space, to spell words that relate to this Scripture passage.

#1 DELDIM

#2 GOFUTH

BOX OF CLUES
STUMPED? MAYBE YOU CAN FIND A CLUE BELOW. (CLUES ARE NOT IN ORDER.)

- The center
- Where Joshua set up camp
- A win or a triumph
- To leave behind
- Battled

#3 LIGLAG

#4 NAABOND

#5 TRIVOYC

MYSTERY ANSWER:
Arrange the circled letters to solve the mystery answer.

A SAD STORY WITH A HAPPY ENDING

RUTH 1–4

Unscramble the Jumbles, one letter to each space, to spell words that relate to this Scripture passage.

#1 BOMA

BOX OF CLUES
STUMPED? MAYBE YOU CAN FIND A CLUE BELOW. (CLUES ARE NOT IN ORDER.)

- The time when crops are gathered
- When an entire area has no food
- A neighboring country to Israel
- Grandfather of King David
- Where crops grow

#2 ODEB

#3 ILFED

#4 NAIMEF

#5 VATESHR

MYSTERY ANSWER:
Arrange the circled letters to solve the mystery answer.

THE ARK IS MISSING!

1 SAMUEL 4–6

Unscramble the Jumbles, one letter to each space, to spell words that relate to this Scripture passage.

#1 VEYHA

BOX OF CLUES

STUMPED? MAYBE YOU CAN FIND A CLUE BELOW. (CLUES ARE NOT IN ORDER.)

- Baby cows
- Deadly curses
- Weighty
- Gave back
- Torn down

#2 VLACSE

#3 LAPGUSE

#4 NEERTUDR

#5 YDROSEDET

MYSTERY ANSWER:

Arrange the circled letters to solve the mystery answer.

THE NEW KING
1 SAMUEL 15:10–16:13

Unscramble the Jumbles, one letter to each space, to spell words that relate to this Scripture passage.

#1 LUSA

BOX OF CLUES
STUMPED? MAYBE YOU CAN FIND A CLUE BELOW. (CLUES ARE NOT IN ORDER.)

- Male family members
- The king before David
- A man who had eight sons
- A purposeful activity
- Poured oil on someone's head; dedicated to service

#2 SEESJ

#3 SISMINO

#4 NONITADE

#5 SHERRBOT

MYSTERY ANSWER:
Arrange the circled letters to solve the mystery answer.

A FURIOUS KING
1 SAMUEL 18:1-16

Unscramble the Jumbles, one letter to each space, to spell words that relate to this Scripture passage.

#1 RHPA

#2 BLASMYC

BOX OF CLUES
STUMPED? MAYBE YOU CAN FIND A CLUE BELOW. (CLUES ARE NOT IN ORDER.)

- David's best pal
- Torturing
- Clanging percussion instruments
- Stringed instrument
- Thriving or prosperous

#3 NAAJOHTN

#4 FUCUSLESSC

#5 NTERGMOTIN

MYSTERY ANSWER:
Arrange the circled letters to solve the mystery answer.

16

A DARING ESCAPE
1 SAMUEL 19–23

Unscramble the Jumbles, one letter to each space, to spell words that relate to this Scripture passage.

#1 DINGIH

BOX OF CLUES
STUMPED? MAYBE YOU CAN FIND A CLUE BELOW. (CLUES ARE NOT IN ORDER.)

- Staying out of sight
- Attacking
- More than hundreds
- To look for something
- Stayed

#2 RSECHA

#3 DIRAGIN

#4 NEEDMIAR

#5 SATSHUDON

MYSTERY ANSWER:
Arrange the circled letters to solve the mystery answer.

17

DAVID REPAYS EVIL WITH GOOD

1 SAMUEL 24

Unscramble the Jumbles, one letter to each space, to spell words that relate to this Scripture passage.

#1 E V A C

BOX OF CLUES

STUMPED? MAYBE YOU CAN FIND A
CLUE BELOW. (CLUES ARE NOT IN ORDER.)

- Opposite of friend
- To hurt
- The area of land governed by royalty
- A rocky den
- Summoned

#2 R A M H

#3 M E E N Y

#4 L E L A D C

#5 D O G M I N K

MYSTERY ANSWER:
Arrange the circled letters to solve the mystery answer.

SAUL'S LAST BATTLE
1 SAMUEL 31

Unscramble the Jumbles, one letter to each space, to spell words that relate to this Scripture passage.

#1 PUCOCIDE

#2 RAWROSIR

BOX OF CLUES
STUMPED? MAYBE YOU CAN FIND A CLUE BELOW. (CLUES ARE NOT IN ORDER.)

- Battling
- Soldiers
- Killed in masses
- Raided
- Taken over by an enemy

#3 TAATKDEC

#4 THINGFIG

#5 TLEEDRASUHG

MYSTERY ANSWER:
Arrange the circled letters to solve the mystery answer.

SOLOMON'S AMAZING BUILDING PROJECT

1 KINGS 8:12–9:14

Unscramble the Jumbles, one letter to each space, to spell words that relate to this Scripture passage.

#1 YOEB

BOX OF CLUES

STUMPED? MAYBE YOU CAN FIND A CLUE BELOW. (CLUES ARE NOT IN ORDER.)

- King of Tyre
- To follow directions
- A festive party
- Happy
- Instructions

#2 IMARH

#3 LUYJOF

#4 MOMACDNS

#5 ETABRONCELI

MYSTERY ANSWER:

Arrange the circled letters to solve the mystery answer.

A WOMAN WITH WEALTH AND SPLENDOR

1 KINGS 10:1-13

Unscramble the Jumbles, one letter to each space, to spell words that relate to this Scripture passage.

#1 BEHSA

#2 WEELJS

BOX OF CLUES

STUMPED? MAYBE YOU CAN FIND A CLUE BELOW. (CLUES ARE NOT IN ORDER.)

- Gems
- Things you ask
- An ancient country in southern Arabia
- Group of travelers
- Fairness

#3 RAACVNA

#4 SUITJEC

#5 SNUTOQISE

MYSTERY ANSWER:
Arrange the circled letters to solve the mystery answer.

A KINGDOM SPLITS IN TWO
1 KINGS 12

Unscramble the Jumbles, one letter to each space, to spell words that relate to this Scripture passage.

#1 BALRO

BOX OF CLUES
STUMPED? MAYBE YOU CAN FIND A CLUE BELOW. (CLUES ARE NOT IN ORDER.)

- Current happenings
- Denied
- Was not willing
- Hard work
- Not southern

#2 TEEVNS

#3 FEESURD

#4 CEEJREDT

#5 NNRROTEH

MYSTERY ANSWER:
Arrange the circled letters to solve the mystery answer.

THE MAN WHO SAW A CHARIOT OF FIRE

2 KINGS 2:1-12

Unscramble the Jumbles, one letter to each space, to spell words that relate to this Scripture passage.

#1 VERIR

BOX OF CLUES

STUMPED? MAYBE YOU CAN FIND A CLUE BELOW. (CLUES ARE NOT IN ORDER.)

- Animals often used for riding
- Immediately
- Speaking
- Tornado-like cloud
- Fast-moving body of water

#2 SHEROS

#3 ALGNTIK

#4 DYNEDULS

#5 NIHLRWIWD

MYSTERY ANSWER:
Arrange the circled letters to solve the mystery answer.

JOASH RESTORES THE HOUSE OF GOD

2 KINGS 12

Unscramble the Jumbles, one letter to each space, to spell words that relate to this Scripture passage.

#1 NYMEO

BOX OF CLUES

STUMPED? MAYBE YOU CAN FIND A CLUE BELOW. (CLUES ARE NOT IN ORDER.)

- Builders and craftsmen
- By choice
- Dollars and cents
- Box for money
- Fixed

#2 SHECT

#3 OMWNREK

#4 REERPDIA

#5 LONUTVARY

MYSTERY ANSWER:
Arrange the circled letters to solve the mystery answer.

A FAITHFUL KING

2 KINGS 18

Unscramble the Jumbles, one letter to each space, to spell words that relate to this Scripture passage.

#1 GINK

BOX OF CLUES

STUMPED? MAYBE YOU CAN FIND A CLUE BELOW. (CLUES ARE NOT IN ORDER.)

- Regal; kingly
- Something that needs to be communicated
- Horse-drawn carriages used in battle
- The king's father
- Ruler of a country

#2 ZAHA

#3 YOLAR

#4 SEAMSEG

#5 CARTSHIO

MYSTERY ANSWER:
Arrange the circled letters to solve the mystery answer.

HEZEKIAH SEEKS GOD'S HELP

2 KINGS 19:14-34

Unscramble the Jumbles, one letter to each space, to spell words that relate to this Scripture passage.

#1 NALPT

BOX OF CLUES

STUMPED? MAYBE YOU CAN FIND A CLUE BELOW. (CLUES ARE NOT IN ORDER.)

- One of Israel's enemies to the north
- To go in
- Protect
- To place seeds in the ground
- A written message you send someone

#2 TEERN

#3 FENDED

#4 TRETEL

#5 RYSASAI

MYSTERY ANSWER:
Arrange the circled letters to solve the mystery answer.

EXTRA YEARS OF LIFE
2 KINGS 20

Unscramble the Jumbles, one letter to each space, to spell words that relate to this Scripture passage.

#1 DOHASW

BOX OF CLUES
STUMPED? MAYBE YOU CAN FIND A CLUE BELOW. (CLUES ARE NOT IN ORDER.)

- One who waits on a master
- A dark figure of something cast by sunlight
- Halfway between ten and twenty
- A helpful oil put on the skin
- Opposite of straight ahead

#2 NFETIEF

#3 TENSVAR

#4 CARBDAWK

#5 MNOTETIN

MYSTERY ANSWER:
Arrange the circled letters to solve the mystery answer.

EVIL IN THE LORD'S SIGHT
2 KINGS 21:1-18

Unscramble the Jumbles, one letter to each space, to spell words that relate to this Scripture passage.

#1 GAPNA

#2 RAAHHSE

#3 TRMANEN

#4 OPPRESTH

#5 SLEETABDET

BOX OF CLUES
STUMPED? MAYBE YOU CAN FIND A CLUE BELOW. (CLUES ARE NOT IN ORDER.)

- Hateful
- Those who speak God's message
- The part left over
- Someone who worships idols
- Ancient pole for idol worship

MYSTERY ANSWER:
Arrange the circled letters to solve the mystery answer.

HARD WORK, GREAT CELEBRATION

EZRA 3:7–4:24

Unscramble the Jumbles, one letter to each space, to spell words that relate to this Scripture passage.

#1 SIPARE

#2 SERUNDE

BOX OF CLUES

STUMPED? MAYBE YOU CAN FIND A CLUE BELOW. (CLUES ARE NOT IN ORDER.)

- Repairing
- Woodworkers
- Lasts a long time
- Cyrus's land
- Formal allowance or consent

#3 GLUDNERIBI

#4 NERTCASPER

#5 SMIPERNOSI

MYSTERY ANSWER:

Arrange the circled letters to solve the mystery answer.

29

A BIG JOB TO DO
NEHEMIAH 2–4

Unscramble the Jumbles, one letter to each space, to spell words that relate to this Scripture passage.

#1 L A L S W

BOX OF CLUES
STUMPED? MAYBE YOU CAN FIND A CLUE BELOW. (CLUES ARE NOT IN ORDER.)

- Swinging entrances
- Not playing
- To look over carefully
- Trash
- Sides of a room

#2 R O S O D

#3 K R O N G I W

#4 P C I T N S E

#5 S U B R B I H

MYSTERY ANSWER:
Arrange the circled letters to solve the mystery answer.

A BRAVE AND BEAUTIFUL QUEEN

ESTHER 1–3

Unscramble the Jumbles, one letter to each space, to spell words that relate to this Scripture passage.

#1 CADIVE

BOX OF CLUES
STUMPED? MAYBE YOU CAN FIND A CLUE BELOW. (CLUES ARE NOT IN ORDER.)

- Suggestion about what to do
- Formal feast
- The queen after Vashti
- Aunt's or uncle's child
- Royal power or greatness

#2 SNIOCU

#3 STREEH

#4 AEJMTYS

#5 QUABTEN

MYSTERY ANSWER:
Arrange the circled letters to solve the mystery answer.

31

SEND ME!

ISAIAH 6

Unscramble the Jumbles, one letter to each space, to spell words that relate to this Scripture passage.

#1 LACO

BOX OF CLUES

STUMPED? MAYBE YOU CAN FIND A CLUE BELOW. (CLUES ARE NOT IN ORDER.)

- One who brings information to another person
- Burning leftover from a fire
- Six-winged angels
- Knowledge of wrongdoing
- The tail of a robe

#2 LGUTI

#3 RNITA

#4 SHARPIME

#5 GERMSESEN

MYSTERY ANSWER:
Arrange the circled letters to solve the mystery answer.

A PROPHET OF DOOM

EZEKIEL 12

Unscramble the Jumbles, one letter to each space, to spell words that relate to this Scripture passage.

#1 LEXIE

BOX OF CLUES
STUMPED? MAYBE YOU CAN FIND A CLUE BELOW. (CLUES ARE NOT IN ORDER.)

- Important city in Israel
- When people are forced out of their homeland
- Prisoners
- A king of Judah who was captured by Babylon
- To spread apart in different directions

#2 CATSRET

#3 DKEHIZEA

#4 SCETIVAP

#5 JAMSUREEL

MYSTERY ANSWER:
Arrange the circled letters to solve the mystery answer.

GET READY TO GO!

EZEKIEL 12

Unscramble the Jumbles, one letter to each space, to spell words that relate to this Scripture passage.

#1 HINGT
◯ ☐ ☐ ☐ ☐

BOX OF CLUES
STUMPED? MAYBE YOU CAN FIND A CLUE BELOW. (CLUES ARE NOT IN ORDER.)

- Traveler's belongings
- Comes after day
- Joint at the top of the arm
- Not the dark of night
- Rule breakers

#2 BEELRS
☐ ☐ ◯ ☐ ◯ ☐

#3 GAABEGG
◯ ☐ ☐ ◯ ☐ ☐ ☐

#4 DEROLUSH
☐ ☐ ◯ ☐ ☐ ☐ ☐ ☐

#5 GALYHIDT
☐ ☐ ◯ ☐ ☐ ☐ ☐ ☐

MYSTERY ANSWER:
Arrange the circled letters to solve the mystery answer.

☐ ☐ ☐ ☐ ☐ ☐ ☐

EZEKIEL'S TOUGH JOB

EZEKIEL 33–34

Unscramble the Jumbles, one letter to each space, to spell words that relate to this Scripture passage.

#1 CEAPE

BOX OF CLUES
STUMPED? MAYBE YOU CAN FIND A CLUE BELOW. (CLUES ARE NOT IN ORDER.)

- A noise to give warning
- Something that indicates danger ahead
- State of rest or quiet
- Animal known for its wool
- Freedom from harm

#2 EPESH

#3 RAMLA

#4 FETYAS

#5 WRINGAN

MYSTERY ANSWER:
Arrange the circled letters to solve the mystery answer.

DANIEL'S SPECIAL GIFT
DANIEL 1–2, 4

Unscramble the Jumbles, one letter to each space, to spell words that relate to this Scripture passage.

#1 LEAVERS

#2 RORSPEP

#3 RYYMEST

#4 TREETIPRN

#5 GRINBUTISD

BOX OF CLUES
STUMPED? MAYBE YOU CAN FIND A CLUE BELOW. (CLUES ARE NOT IN ORDER.)

- A detective unravels this
- To succeed
- Bothersome
- To give the meaning of something
- Makes known; shows

MYSTERY ANSWER:
Arrange the circled letters to solve the mystery answer.

FROM ABRAHAM TO JESUS

MATTHEW 1:1-17

Unscramble the Jumbles, one letter to each space, to spell words that relate to this Scripture passage.

#1 ZABO

BOX OF CLUES
STUMPED? MAYBE YOU CAN FIND A CLUE BELOW. (CLUES ARE NOT IN ORDER.)

- Fishy Old Testament name
- Mother of Solomon
- Mother of Perez and Zerah
- Son of Rahab
- Son of Isaac

#2 CAJBO

#3 MATAR

#4 AMSNOL

#5 SETHBABHA

MYSTERY ANSWER:
Arrange the circled letters to solve the mystery answer.

THE WISE MEN'S QUEST
MATTHEW 2:9-12

Unscramble the Jumbles, one letter to each space, to spell words that relate to this Scripture passage.

#1 LOGD

BOX OF CLUES
STUMPED? MAYBE YOU CAN FIND A CLUE BELOW. (CLUES ARE NOT IN ORDER.)

- Strong-smelling oil the wise men brought
- Led
- Presented
- Yellowish metal
- Large treasure boxes

#2 VEAG

#3 RHYMR

#4 DDUGEI

#5 TSSEHC

MYSTERY ANSWER:
Arrange the circled letters to solve the mystery answer.

ESCAPE IN THE NIGHT

MATTHEW 2:13-18

Unscramble the Jumbles, one letter to each space, to spell words that relate to this Scripture passage.

#1 RAMY

BOX OF CLUES

STUMPED? MAYBE YOU CAN FIND A CLUE BELOW. (CLUES ARE NOT IN ORDER.)

- A messenger from God
- Earthly father of Jesus
- Jesus' mother
- To come back
- Cries

#2 EWPES

#3 GANLE

#4 NURTER

#5 SHEPJO

MYSTERY ANSWER:
Arrange the circled letters to solve the mystery answer.

39

A STRANGE JOB
FOR A FISH
MATTHEW 17:24-27

Unscramble the Jumbles, one letter to each space, to spell words that relate to this Scripture passage.

#1 SEY

BOX OF CLUES
STUMPED? MAYBE YOU CAN FIND A CLUE BELOW. (CLUES ARE NOT IN ORDER.)

- Those who gather money or other objects from people
- To trap fish
- Word used to show agreement
- Jewish place of worship
- People in a city or town

#2 HACTC

#3 METPEL

#4 EICZISNT

#5 SECTCOLLOR

MYSTERY ANSWER:
Arrange the circled letters to solve the mystery answer.

JESUS, THE STORYTELLER

MATTHEW 18–22

Unscramble the Jumbles, one letter to each space, to spell words that relate to this Scripture passage.

#1 STOL

BOX OF CLUES

STUMPED? MAYBE YOU CAN FIND A CLUE BELOW. (CLUES ARE NOT IN ORDER.)

- Creatures that say "baa"
- Grape field
- Those who owe money
- Unable to find the way
- People who grow crops for a living

#2 PEESH

#3 MARFSER

#4 TRESDOB

#5 RINYEVDA

MYSTERY ANSWER:
Arrange the circled letters to solve the mystery answer.

A MIRACLE BY JESUS
MATTHEW 20:29-34

Unscramble the Jumbles, one letter to each space, to spell words that relate to this Scripture passage.

#1 N W T A

BOX OF CLUES
STUMPED? MAYBE YOU CAN FIND A CLUE BELOW. (CLUES ARE NOT IN ORDER.)

- Came behind
- Close followers of Jesus
- Halted
- Started
- To desire

#2 G N E B A

#3 P O P E S D T

#4 W O O L L E F D

#5 S L E D P I C S I

MYSTERY ANSWER:
Arrange the circled letters to solve the mystery answer.

THREE SERVANTS

MATTHEW 25:14-30

Unscramble the Jumbles, one letter to each space, to spell words that relate to this Scripture passage.

#1 NEARVST

BOX OF CLUES

STUMPED? MAYBE YOU CAN FIND A CLUE BELOW. (CLUES ARE NOT IN ORDER.)

- To care for
- Someone who reports to his or her master
- Trustworthy
- Gave responsibility to
- Without purpose; unwilling to help

#2 SLEESUS

#3 FITHULFA

#4 STEDTRNUE

#5 VELTATUCI

MYSTERY ANSWER:
Arrange the circled letters to solve the mystery answer.

43

A NIGHT OF PRAYER

MATTHEW 26:36-46

Unscramble the Jumbles, one letter to each space, to spell words that relate to this Scripture passage.

#1 OCEM

BOX OF CLUES
STUMPED? MAYBE YOU CAN FIND A
CLUE BELOW. (CLUES ARE NOT IN ORDER.)

- Extreme sadness
- Look for
- Not go
- Those who do wrong
- Turned over to the enemy

#2 FERGI

#3 HAWCT

#4 RNINSES

#5 RATBEDEY

MYSTERY ANSWER:
Arrange the circled letters to solve the mystery answer.

PUTTING JESUS ON TRIAL

MATTHEW 27:11-26

Unscramble the Jumbles, one letter to each space, to spell words that relate to this Scripture passage.

#1 NMROA

BOX OF CLUES

STUMPED? MAYBE YOU CAN FIND A CLUE BELOW. (CLUES ARE NOT IN ORDER.)

- Accusations
- Person in jail
- Religious leaders
- Shouted
- The soldiers' citizenship

#2 LEELDY

#3 GRASCHE

#4 TRIPSES

#5 SPORENRI

MYSTERY ANSWER:
Arrange the circled letters to solve the mystery answer.

SOLDIERS MAKE FUN OF JESUS

MATTHEW 27:27-31

Unscramble the Jumbles, one letter to each space, to spell words that relate to this Scripture passage.

#1 YAAW

BOX OF CLUES
STUMPED? MAYBE YOU CAN FIND A CLUE BELOW. (CLUES ARE NOT IN ORDER.)

- Military unit
- Royal accessory
- Bent one's knees
- Somewhere else
- Tree limbs

#2 LENTK

#3 WROCN

#4 MINTGERE

#5 NREBAHSC

MYSTERY ANSWER:
Arrange the circled letters to solve the mystery answer.

THE DARKEST DAY

MATTHEW 27:32-44

Unscramble the Jumbles, one letter to each space, to spell words that relate to this Scripture passage.

#1 RUGDA

BOX OF CLUES

STUMPED? MAYBE YOU CAN FIND A CLUE BELOW. (CLUES ARE NOT IN ORDER.)

- Mocked; scorned
- Where a man named Simon was from
- Wooden stake with an intersecting beam
- Shamed; teased harshly
- To keep watch over

#2 SCSOR

#3 REEYNC

#4 FOFSEDC

#5 DIRULEDIC

MYSTERY ANSWER:
Arrange the circled letters to solve the mystery answer.

JESUS AMAZES THE CROWD

MARK 1:21-28

Unscramble the Jumbles, one letter to each space, to spell words that relate to this Scripture passage.

#1 TIQUE

BOX OF CLUES

STUMPED? MAYBE YOU CAN FIND A CLUE BELOW. (CLUES ARE NOT IN ORDER.)

- The last day of the week
- To wreck; ruin
- Not loud
- Screaming
- Commands

#2 RODERS

#3 TABBSAH

#4 YORDSTE

#5 NUSIOHTG

MYSTERY ANSWER:
Arrange the circled letters to solve the mystery answer.

MIRACLE FOR A DEAF MAN

MARK 7:31-37

Unscramble the Jumbles, one letter to each space, to spell words that relate to this Scripture passage.

#1 CPHESE

BOX OF CLUES

STUMPED? MAYBE YOU CAN FIND A CLUE BELOW. (CLUES ARE NOT IN ORDER.)

- Ejecting saliva from the mouth
- Pleaded
- Communication by mouth
- Parts of the body at the end of the hand
- Clearly

#2 GEEGDB

#3 LILAPYN

#4 SIFRENG

#5 INGTIPST

MYSTERY ANSWER:
Arrange the circled letters to solve the mystery answer.

HOW TO BE FIRST IN GOD'S KINGDOM

MARK 9:33-37

Unscramble the Jumbles, one letter to each space, to spell words that relate to this Scripture passage.

#1 SLAT

BOX OF CLUES

STUMPED? MAYBE YOU CAN FIND A CLUE BELOW. (CLUES ARE NOT IN ORDER.)

- Small
- Talking about
- City where Jesus and his followers stayed
- Place to live
- At the end

#2 OSEHU

#3 TELLIT

#4 ACPMAENUR

#5 SNICUSIDSG

MYSTERY ANSWER:

Arrange the circled letters to solve the mystery answer.

THE MOST IMPORTANT RULE

MARK 12:28-34

Unscramble the Jumbles, one letter to each space, to spell words that relate to this Scripture passage.

#1 VEOL

BOX OF CLUES

STUMPED? MAYBE YOU CAN FIND A CLUE BELOW. (CLUES ARE NOT IN ORDER.)

- Someone who lives nearby
- Might; power
- Hearing
- Replied
- Strong affection

#2 GIRNHOBE

#3 SREANEWD

#4 TEGRHNST

#5 NISLIGENT

MYSTERY ANSWER:
Arrange the circled letters to solve the mystery answer.

JESUS CELEBRATES PASSOVER

MARK 14:12-26

Unscramble the Jumbles, one letter to each space, to spell words that relate to this Scripture passage.

#1 EBTRYA

BOX OF CLUES
STUMPED? MAYBE YOU CAN FIND A CLUE BELOW. (CLUES ARE NOT IN ORDER.)

- Gave God's grace
- What Judas would do to Jesus
- Emptied
- To get ready
- Bits or segments

#2 ROPUED

#3 SCEEIP

#4 DLSESEB

#5 REERPPA

MYSTERY ANSWER:
Arrange the circled letters to solve the mystery answer.

ZECHARIAH'S BIG MISTAKE

LUKE 1:5-25

Unscramble the Jumbles, one letter to each space, to spell words that relate to this Scripture passage.

#1 TARAL

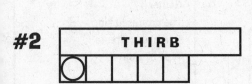

BOX OF CLUES

STUMPED? MAYBE YOU CAN FIND A CLUE BELOW. (CLUES ARE NOT IN ORDER.)

- Where sacrifices are offered
- Scared
- A burning fragrance
- Joy
- The start of a life

#2 THIRB

#3 RADIFA

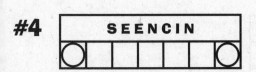

#4 SEENCIN

#5 NLDAGSES

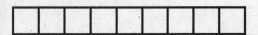

MYSTERY ANSWER:

Arrange the circled letters to solve the mystery answer.

JOHN THE BAPTIST'S PULPIT

LUKE 3:1-20

Unscramble the Jumbles, one letter to each space, to spell words that relate to this Scripture passage.

#1 HATEW

BOX OF CLUES

STUMPED? MAYBE YOU CAN FIND A CLUE BELOW. (CLUES ARE NOT IN ORDER.)

- Alarms
- Gather
- The promised king
- To make; to create
- Type of grain

#2 CLLCETO

#3 DRPUECO

#4 SHAIMES

#5 NNARWGIS

MYSTERY ANSWER:
Arrange the circled letters to solve the mystery answer.

A WOMAN SHOWS HER LOVE

LUKE 7:36-50

Unscramble the Jumbles, one letter to each space, to spell words that relate to this Scripture passage.

#1 INSS

#2 VESDA

#3 DOLNAE

#4 FEERMUP

#5 INKELNGE

BOX OF CLUES
STUMPED? MAYBE YOU CAN FIND A CLUE BELOW. (CLUES ARE NOT IN ORDER.)

- Wrongdoings
- Bending the knees
- Allowed someone to borrow
- Fragrance
- Rescued

MYSTERY ANSWER:
Arrange the circled letters to solve the mystery answer.

55

JESUS MEETS THE KNOW-IT-ALLS

LUKE 11:37-54

Unscramble the Jumbles, one letter to each space, to spell words that relate to this Scripture passage.

#1 REEPTX

#2 YLIFHT

#3 CLEEGNT

#4 NWAGIHS

#5 SILNTUDE

BOX OF CLUES

STUMPED? MAYBE YOU CAN FIND A CLUE BELOW. (CLUES ARE NOT IN ORDER.)

- Criticized
- Really dirty
- To ignore
- Cleansing
- Someone who knows a lot about a topic

MYSTERY ANSWER:
Arrange the circled letters to solve the mystery answer.

JESUS' SABBATH MIRACLE
LUKE 14:1-6

Unscramble the Jumbles, one letter to each space, to spell words that relate to this Scripture passage.

#1 SLEG

BOX OF CLUES
STUMPED? MAYBE YOU CAN FIND A CLUE BELOW. (CLUES ARE NOT IN ORDER.)

- Puffy; bloated
- To respond
- Not breakfast or lunch
- Felt
- Parts of the body that help you walk

#2 NINRED

#3 WRENSA

#4 HOTUDEC

#5 LWOSNEL

MYSTERY ANSWER:
Arrange the circled letters to solve the mystery answer.

THE ONE WHO SAID THANK YOU

LUKE 17:11-19

Unscramble the Jumbles, one letter to each space, to spell words that relate to this Scripture passage.

#1 RECYM

BOX OF CLUES

STUMPED? MAYBE YOU CAN FIND A CLUE BELOW. (CLUES ARE NOT IN ORDER.)

- Honor or praise
- To tell how wonderful someone is
- Washed
- Grace
- Boundary

#2 ROLGY

#3 EPIRSA

#4 REROBD

#5 DLEESANC

MYSTERY ANSWER:

Arrange the circled letters to solve the mystery answer.

HE IS RISEN!

LUKE 24:1-12

Unscramble the Jumbles, one letter to each space, to spell words that relate to this Scripture passage.

#1 RITHD

BOX OF CLUES
STUMPED? MAYBE YOU CAN FIND A CLUE BELOW. (CLUES ARE NOT IN ORDER.)

- Between second and fourth
- Hurried
- Not full
- Dressed
- When the sun arrives

#2 TYMPE

#3 HREUDS

#4 NNOMIGR

#5 TOLCDEH

MYSTERY ANSWER:
Arrange the circled letters to solve the mystery answer.

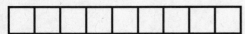

NEVER THIRSTY AGAIN

JOHN 4:1-38

Unscramble the Jumbles, one letter to each space, to spell words that relate to this Scripture passage.

#1 LEWL

#2 SREFH

BOX OF CLUES

STUMPED? MAYBE YOU CAN FIND A CLUE BELOW. (CLUES ARE NOT IN ORDER.)

- Pail
- What is right and real
- Male spouse
- Not frozen or old
- Spring for water

#3 TTRUH

#4 KTBEUC

#5 NUHBSDA

MYSTERY ANSWER:
Arrange the circled letters to solve the mystery answer.

MIRACLE FOR A LAME MAN

JOHN 5:1-15

Unscramble the Jumbles, one letter to each space, to spell words that relate to this Scripture passage.

#1
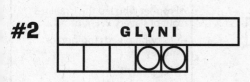
KISC

BOX OF CLUES

STUMPED? MAYBE YOU CAN FIND A CLUE BELOW. (CLUES ARE NOT IN ORDER.)

- Reclining
- Unhealthy
- Pool where a miracle took place
- Forms air pockets in the water
- Liquid in a pool

#2

GLYNI

#3
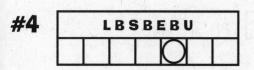
TERAW

#4

LBSBEBU

#5
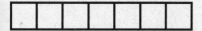
SEEDABHT

MYSTERY ANSWER:
Arrange the circled letters to solve the mystery answer.

JESUS SHOWS WHAT HIS FATHER IS LIKE

JOHN 9

Unscramble the Jumbles, one letter to each space, to spell words that relate to this Scripture passage.

#1 SEOMS

#2 TRBIH

#3 GEBRGA

#4 MALOIS

#5 YIGNRT

BOX OF CLUES

STUMPED? MAYBE YOU CAN FIND A CLUE BELOW. (CLUES ARE NOT IN ORDER.)

- First entrance into the world
- Attempting
- Prophet who led the Israelites out of slavery in Egypt
- One who pleads for food or money
- Means "sent"

MYSTERY ANSWER:
Arrange the circled letters to solve the mystery answer.

JESUS KNOWS HIS FLOCK

JOHN 10:11-18

Unscramble the Jumbles, one letter to each space, to spell words that relate to this Scripture passage.

#1 CEVIO

BOX OF CLUES

STUMPED? MAYBE YOU CAN FIND A CLUE BELOW. (CLUES ARE NOT IN ORDER.)

- Power or right to rule
- Spreads around
- Sound that comes from the mouth
- Pen or shelter for lambs
- To give something up by choice

#2 ARESTCTS

#3 CRISIFACE

#4 FLOPHESED

#5 HUYRIATOT

MYSTERY ANSWER:

Arrange the circled letters to solve the mystery answer.

63

JESUS SERVES HIS FRIENDS

JOHN 13:1-17

Unscramble the Jumbles, one letter to each space, to spell words that relate to this Scripture passage.

#1 SABNI

BOX OF CLUES

STUMPED? MAYBE YOU CAN FIND A CLUE BELOW. (CLUES ARE NOT IN ORDER.)

- Piece of cloth used for drying
- One who instructs students
- Party
- Sink or washtub
- To be part of a group

#2 WOLET

#3 NEBLOG

#4 HATCEER

#5 NOBRECATILE

MYSTERY ANSWER:
Arrange the circled letters to solve the mystery answer.

ONE GLORIOUS MORNING

JOHN 20:1-10

Unscramble the Jumbles, one letter to each space, to spell words that relate to this Scripture passage.

#1

LEYRA

BOX OF CLUES

STUMPED? MAYBE YOU CAN FIND A CLUE BELOW. (CLUES ARE NOT IN ORDER.)

- One who follows Jesus
- Moved faster
- Near the beginning
- Spun
- Within

#2

DISINE

#3

LOLRDE

#4

NUTAOR

#5

CLIPSIDE

MYSTERY ANSWER:
Arrange the circled letters to solve the mystery answer.

65

"WHY ARE YOU CRYING?"

JOHN 20:11-29

Unscramble the Jumbles, one letter to each space, to spell words that relate to this Scripture passage.

#1 C E P E A

BOX OF CLUES

STUMPED? MAYBE YOU CAN FIND A CLUE BELOW. (CLUES ARE NOT IN ORDER.)

- Where mittens go
- You point with this
- Calm; rest
- Location
- To have faith

#2 D S N A H

#3 L C P A E

#4 G R I N F E

#5 L E E V I B E

MYSTERY ANSWER:
Arrange the circled letters to solve the mystery answer.

A MIGHTY MOVEMENT OF GOD

ACTS 2:1-13

Unscramble the Jumbles, one letter to each space, to spell words that relate to this Scripture passage.

#1 DRCWO

BOX OF CLUES

STUMPED? MAYBE YOU CAN FIND A CLUE BELOW. (CLUES ARE NOT IN ORDER.)

- Skill
- Not body
- Talking
- Large gathering of people
- All the people

#2 TRISIP

#3 LITYIBA

#4 NREEYOEV

#5 PKGSNIAE

MYSTERY ANSWER:

Arrange the circled letters to solve the mystery answer.

A CHRISTIAN COMMUNITY

ACTS 2:42-47

Unscramble the Jumbles, one letter to each space, to spell words that relate to this Scripture passage.

#1 SMOEH

BOX OF CLUES

STUMPED? MAYBE YOU CAN FIND A CLUE BELOW. (CLUES ARE NOT IN ORDER.)

- Capacity for giving to others
- Buildings where people live
- Instructing
- A feeling of friendship and community
- Supernatural

#2 CHINETAG

#3 CURSIMOULA

#4 PLIFSLOWEH

#5 TORSYGEENI

MYSTERY ANSWER:

Arrange the circled letters to solve the mystery answer.

PETER'S STRANGE EXPERIENCE

ACTS 10:9-33

Unscramble the Jumbles, one letter to each space, to spell words that relate to this Scripture passage.

#1 NASDT

BOX OF CLUES

STUMPED? MAYBE YOU CAN FIND A CLUE BELOW. (CLUES ARE NOT IN ORDER.)

- Asked to come
- Creatures
- Reverent; faithful
- Yucky; dirty
- What you do on your feet

#2 TEUDOV

#3 NUCEANL

#4 SMAINAL

#5 TINIEVD

MYSTERY ANSWER:

Arrange the circled letters to solve the mystery answer.

A MIRACULOUS ESCAPE

ACTS 12:6-19

Unscramble the Jumbles, one letter to each space, to spell words that relate to this Scripture passage.

#1 LECL

BOX OF CLUES

STUMPED? MAYBE YOU CAN FIND A CLUE BELOW. (CLUES ARE NOT IN ORDER.)

- A room in prison
- Tapped loudly
- Wits
- Illuminated; full of light
- Not running

#2 RGBITH

#3 SEESNS

#4 CONKKDE

#5 GNALIKW

MYSTERY ANSWER:
Arrange the circled letters to solve the mystery answer.

THE IMPORTANT MEETING
ACTS 15

Unscramble the Jumbles, one letter to each space, to spell words that relate to this Scripture passage.

#1 RHHUCC

BOX OF CLUES
STUMPED? MAYBE YOU CAN FIND A
CLUE BELOW. (CLUES ARE NOT IN ORDER.)

- Completed
- Told the Good News
- Deal with successfully
- People who have been changed by Jesus
- Gathering of God's people

#2 VREELSO

#3 DRAHEEPC

#4 HINDIFES

#5 TRONEVCS

MYSTERY ANSWER:
Arrange the circled letters to solve the mystery answer.

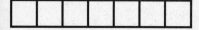

PAUL IS CAPTURED

ACTS 21:30–23:35

Unscramble the Jumbles, one letter to each space, to spell words that relate to this Scripture passage.

#1 CRFOE

BOX OF CLUES

STUMPED? MAYBE YOU CAN FIND A CLUE BELOW. (CLUES ARE NOT IN ORDER.)

- Argument
- Jewish religious leader in New Testament times
- People belonging to a group
- Physical strength
- Relatives from past generations

#2 BEMMRSE

#3 CCLTNOIF

#4 HESIPREA

#5 TRNSSACOE

MYSTERY ANSWER:

Arrange the circled letters to solve the mystery answer.

PAUL'S IMPORTANT TEACHINGS

ROMANS 12–14

Unscramble the Jumbles, one letter to each space, to spell words that relate to this Scripture passage.

#1 EEVRS

BOX OF CLUES

STUMPED? MAYBE YOU CAN FIND A CLUE BELOW. (CLUES ARE NOT IN ORDER.)

- Belief
- One who holds to the faith
- To do something for others
- Not one bit of anything
- To become something new

#2 FIHAT

#3 GONNIHT

#4 LIBERVEE

#5 SORTNFARM

MYSTERY ANSWER:

Arrange the circled letters to solve the mystery answer.

A REQUEST FOR UNITY

PHILEMON 1

Unscramble the Jumbles, one letter to each space, to spell words that relate to this Scripture passage.

#1 DOCRFE

#2 GONPIH

BOX OF CLUES

STUMPED? MAYBE YOU CAN FIND A CLUE BELOW. (CLUES ARE NOT IN ORDER.)

- Made to do something
- To bring up in conversation
- To greet or invite in
- Peer; also another word for "guy"
- Wishing

#3 LOLWEF

#4 CLOWMEE

#5 TOMNIEN

MYSTERY ANSWER:
Arrange the circled letters to solve the mystery answer.

JOHN'S AMAZING VISION

REVELATION 4–6

Unscramble the Jumbles, one letter to each space, to spell words that relate to this Scripture passage.

#1

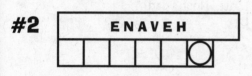
VENES

BOX OF CLUES

STUMPED? MAYBE YOU CAN FIND A CLUE BELOW. (CLUES ARE NOT IN ORDER.)

- God's kingdom
- Valuable; important
- Brass instrument
- Colorful arch
- Symbolic number that comes up often in Revelation

#2

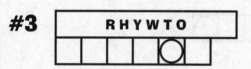
ENAVEH

#3

RHYWTO

#4

MRETTUP

#5

NIRWOBA

MYSTERY ANSWER:

Arrange the circled letters to solve the mystery answer.

SOMEONE WITH A LONG LIFE

GENESIS 5

Unscramble the Jumbles, one letter to each space, to spell words that relate to the mystery person.

#1 N A M U H   CLUE: Man or woman

#2 M A H L C E   CLUE: Noah's dad

#3 G U T S A D E H R   CLUE: Female offspring

#4 R E Y A S   CLUE: Annual periods of time

#5 N E O H C   CLUE: A man who walked with God

MYSTERY PERSON:
Arrange the circled letters to solve the mystery person.

THE FIRST OF GOD'S CHOSEN PEOPLE

GENESIS 15–18

Unscramble the Jumbles, one letter to each space, to spell words that relate to the mystery person.

#1 WARDER CLUE: Prize

#2 RAAHS CLUE: Abram's wife's new name

#3 STRAS CLUE: Natural night-lights

#4 VEEDIBEL CLUE: Accepted as true

#5 SIMORPED CLUE: Made a firm commitment

MYSTERY PERSON:
Arrange the circled letters to solve the mystery person.

A DREAMER WHO FINDS ADVENTURE

GENESIS 37; 39–41

Unscramble the Jumbles, one letter to each space, to spell words that relate to the mystery person.

#1 CAJBO

CLUE: Man with twelve sons

#2 LAMSEC

CLUE: Desert animals with one or two humps

#3 RTSBEROH

CLUE: Male relatives

#4 SRUPTEA

CLUE: Grassland for animals

#5 SARTS

CLUE: Twinkling lights in the sky

MYSTERY PERSON:

Arrange the circled letters to solve the mystery person.

A PROPHET WHO SANG

EXODUS 2; 15

Unscramble the Jumbles, one letter to each space, to spell words that relate to the mystery person.

#1 STREIS CLUE: Female relative

#2 DAIM CLUE: Young woman servant

#3 SOSME CLUE: Israelite leader

#4 NADDEC CLUE: Moved to a rhythm

#5 TROPPHE CLUE: Person who speaks for God

MYSTERY PERSON:
Arrange the circled letters to solve the mystery person.

A STUBBORN RULER
EXODUS 7–10

Unscramble the Jumbles, one letter to each space, to spell words that relate to the mystery person.

#1 T F F A S

CLUE: Aaron's walking stick

#2 I L A H

CLUE: Falling ice cubes

#3 R R V I E

CLUE: Nile or Jordan

#4 T R E P N E S

CLUE: Snake

#5 S H E S R O

CLUE: Animals controlled by reins

MYSTERY PERSON:
Arrange the circled letters to solve the mystery person.

A BRAVE YOUNG LEADER

JOSHUA 6

Unscramble the Jumbles, one letter to each space, to spell words that relate to the mystery person.

#1 RRORIWAS

CLUE: Those who fight

#2 ORANDU

CLUE: Along the circumference

#3 HRCIJOE

CLUE: Walled city

#4 SLACOLEP

CLUE: Fall down

#5 CRAMH

CLUE: To walk in step with others

MYSTERY PERSON:

Arrange the circled letters to solve the mystery person.

A FARMER WHO IS CALLED TO FIGHT

JUDGES 6–7

Unscramble the Jumbles, one letter to each space, to spell words that relate to the mystery person.

#1 `SJAHO`

CLUE: A man from the clan of Abiezer

#2 `CLEFEE`

CLUE: A sheep's coat

#3 `TRIVYCO`

CLUE: A win in battle

#4 `GUDJE`

CLUE: Someone who decides the case

#5 `TIMDHING`

CLUE: 12:00 a.m.

MYSTERY PERSON:

Arrange the circled letters to solve the mystery person.

A STRONG MAN IN TROUBLE

JUDGES 13–16

Unscramble the Jumbles, one letter to each space, to spell words that relate to the mystery person.

#1 NOLI

CLUE: Not-so-cuddly cat

#2 WODEV

CLUE: Promised

#3 RIHA

CLUE: What grows on your head

#4 WRASM

CLUE: Large number of insects

#5 SKROE

CLUE: Delilah's home

MYSTERY PERSON:
Arrange the circled letters to solve the mystery person.

A PRAYING MOTHER
1 SAMUEL 1–2

Unscramble the Jumbles, one letter to each space, to spell words that relate to the mystery person.

#1 LIHHOS — CLUE: Village of worship in the Old Testament

#2 KABEST — CLUE: Woven container

#3 KAANELH — CLUE: Samuel's father

#4 TRGNA — CLUE: Give

#5 DENEY — CLUE: Desperate; in want of support

MYSTERY PERSON:
Arrange the circled letters to solve the mystery person.

84

A GODLY BOY
1 SAMUEL 3

Unscramble the Jumbles, one letter to each space, to spell words that relate to the mystery person.

#1 SPINGELE CLUE: Resting in bed

#2 GUDMNETJ CLUE: What is fair based on the evidence

#3 BEELLARI CLUE: Dependable

#4 GAMSSEES CLUE: Notes that are sent to someone

#5 SETHRAT CLUE: Warnings

MYSTERY PERSON:
Arrange the circled letters to solve the mystery person.

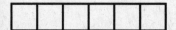

85

MYSTERY PERSON #11

AN ENORMOUS ENEMY
1 SAMUEL 17

Unscramble the Jumbles, one letter to each space, to spell words that relate to the mystery person.

#1 I V F E
CLUE: A handful

#2 D R O A F E H E
CLUE: Area above the eyebrows

#3 P E M O C T T N
CLUE: Disrespect

#4 T G N I A
CLUE: Extremely tall person

#5 B E L T M U D S
CLUE: Tripped

MYSTERY PERSON:
Arrange the circled letters to solve the mystery person.

86

THE KING WHO HAD IT ALL
1 KINGS 1–11

Unscramble the Jumbles, one letter to each space, to spell words that relate to the mystery person.

#1 GDOL   CLUE: Valuable metal

#2 PLEETM   CLUE: God's house

#3 SNITONA   CLUE: Countries

#4 RAYOL   CLUE: Kingly

#5 MOSDWI   CLUE: Godly insight

MYSTERY PERSON:
Arrange the circled letters to solve the mystery person.

A POWERFUL PROPHET
1 KINGS 17–22

Unscramble the Jumbles, one letter to each space, to spell words that relate to the mystery person.

#1 N E R V A S
CLUE: Black birds

#2 D I W O W
CLUE: Woman whose husband died

#3 S A L I H E
CLUE: The prophet's successor

#4 O N D J A R
CLUE: River in Israel

#5 P C D M E A
CLUE: Slept in a tent

MYSTERY PERSON:
Arrange the circled letters to solve the mystery person.

PROPHET WITH A DOUBLE BLESSING

2 KINGS 1–2

Unscramble the Jumbles, one letter to each space, to spell words that relate to the mystery person.

#1 VERIR CLUE: Flowing stream

#2 TIRINEH CLUE: To receive after someone's death

#3 STAMER CLUE: One who has servants

#4 BOLDUE CLUE: Twice as much

#5 KOLAC CLUE: Overcoat

MYSTERY PERSON:
Arrange the circled letters to solve the mystery person.

A YOUNG KING OF JUDAH
2 KINGS 15:1-8

Unscramble the Jumbles, one letter to each space, to spell words that relate to the mystery person.

#1 ARAZHECIH   CLUE: A king of Israel

#2 ZAAMHIA   CLUE: The previous king of Judah

#3 TEXESIN   CLUE: Four times four

#4 NERBUD   CLUE: Went up in flames

#5 MAJTHO   CLUE: The next king of Judah

MYSTERY PERSON:
Arrange the circled letters to solve the mystery person.

A GODLY KING
2 CHRONICLES 17–18

Unscramble the Jumbles, one letter to each space, to spell words that relate to the mystery person.

#1
DAJHU

CLUE: The southern kingdom

#2
HARTFE

CLUE: Dad

#3
POORTS

CLUE: Military units

#4
HIMIAAC

CLUE: One of God's prophets

#5
SESTRSEFOR

CLUE: Places of protection from the enemy

MYSTERY PERSON:
Arrange the circled letters to solve the mystery person.

A WOMAN WHO RESCUED GOD'S PEOPLE

ESTHER 7–10

Unscramble the Jumbles, one letter to each space, to spell words that relate to the mystery person.

#1 QTNABEU

CLUE: Elaborate meal

#2 MNAAH

CLUE: An enemy of the Jews who got a taste of his own medicine

#3 RIUPM

CLUE: A Jewish holiday

#4 ODECIMAR

CLUE: A godly man who took care of his cousin

#5 NADSELGS

CLUE: Happiness

MYSTERY PERSON:
Arrange the circled letters to solve the mystery person.

A BRAVE FRIEND
DANIEL 1–3

Unscramble the Jumbles, one letter to each space, to spell words that relate to the mystery person.

#1 SLFMAE

CLUE: Tongues of fire

#2 DIMENETRED

CLUE: Set on doing something

#3 RAAHHCSD

CLUE: Fellow captive

#4 LOBBNYA

CLUE: Nebuchadnezzar's empire

#5 UCAENFR

CLUE: Where he had a hot time

MYSTERY PERSON:
Arrange the circled letters to solve the mystery person.

A NEW TESTAMENT PROPHET

MATTHEW 11:1-19

Unscramble the Jumbles, one letter to each space, to spell words that relate to the mystery person.

#1 SUJES   CLUE: God's son

#2 VEANHE   CLUE: God's kingdom

#3 TOINSCUSIRTN   CLUE: Directions

#4 NILBD   CLUE: Unable to see

#5 THROPPE   CLUE: God's delivery person

MYSTERY PERSON:
Arrange the circled letters to solve the mystery person.

ONE WHO WASHED HIS HANDS

MATTHEW 27:11-26

Unscramble the Jumbles, one letter to each space, to spell words that relate to the mystery person.

#1 TRESPIS

CLUE: Jewish religious leaders

#2 CONENITN

CLUE: Not guilty

#3 SIPURERS

CLUE: Something unexpected

#4 SEALEER

CLUE: To let go

#5 GLOGDEF

CLUE: Whipped

MYSTERY PERSON:

Arrange the circled letters to solve the mystery person.

A MAN IN A TREE

LUKE 18:35–19:10

Unscramble the Jumbles, one letter to each space, to spell words that relate to the mystery person.

#1 SUTEG

CLUE: Someone who comes over for dinner

#2 XSATE

CLUE: Money for the government

#3 THACEED

CLUE: Tricked

#4 ZENERANA

CLUE: A person from Jesus' hometown

#5 MOAREYCS

CLUE: A tree that can easily be climbed

MYSTERY PERSON:
Arrange the circled letters to solve the mystery person.

A NIGHTTIME VISITOR

JOHN 3

Unscramble the Jumbles, one letter to each space, to spell words that relate to the mystery person.

#1 NIVEGEN

CLUE: Twilight

#2 MOKIGND

CLUE: Royal territory

#3 THUTR

CLUE: Not a lie

#4 ATRIPSULI

CLUE: Of the soul

#5 CUULOSMRIA

CLUE: Seemingly impossible

MYSTERY PERSON:
Arrange the circled letters to solve the mystery person.

A BROTHER WHO GETS A SECOND CHANCE

JOHN 11

Unscramble the Jumbles, one letter to each space, to spell words that relate to the mystery person.

#1 MELSL

CLUE: Odor

#2 NEBAYHT

CLUE: Hometown of Mary and Martha

#3 AGEVR

CLUE: Burial place

#4 PRUWNA

CLUE: Remove a covering

#5 ZEARILE

CLUE: To become aware

MYSTERY PERSON:

Arrange the circled letters to solve the mystery person.

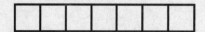

98

A MAN WHO STRETCHED THE TRUTH

ACTS 5:1-11

Unscramble the Jumbles, one letter to each space, to spell words that relate to the mystery person.

#1 NILYG

CLUE: Saying something that isn't true

#2 GIMLACIN

CLUE: Declaring

#3 NOYEM

CLUE: How you pay for things

#4 LILGENS

CLUE: Exchanging something for money

#5 HAAPIPRS

CLUE: Woman who sold some property with her husband

MYSTERY PERSON:

Arrange the circled letters to solve the mystery person.

SOMEONE IN THE RIGHT PLACE AT THE RIGHT TIME

ACTS 8:26-40

Unscramble the Jumbles, one letter to each space, to spell words that relate to the mystery person.

#1 KOLO

CLUE: See

#2 PITIHOAE

CLUE: Country in Africa

#3 RRIPUTSEC

CLUE: The Word of God

#4 ZEPIBADT

CLUE: Spiritually dunked

#5 GARIRACE

CLUE: Horse-drawn vehicle

MYSTERY PERSON:
Arrange the circled letters to solve the mystery person.

THE CASE OF THE OVERARCHING PROMISE

GENESIS 9:1-17

Unscramble the Jumbles, one letter to each space, to spell words as suggested by the trivia clues.

#1 What's another way to say "gave divine favor"?

SLEDEBS

#2 What are "cirrus" and "stratus" examples of?

CLUSOD

#3 What is a sacred agreement?

NNVATEOC

#4 What is it when you verify the truth?

MROCIFN

#5 What are raging rapids that come after a big storm?

TRODLAWFOES

MYSTERY QUESTION:
Arrange the circled letters to answer the mystery question.

What is a symbol of God's promise that he will never again flood the entire earth?

THE CASE OF THE BROTHERS' BETRAYAL

GENESIS 37:18-36

Unscramble the Jumbles, one letter to each space, to spell words as suggested by the trivia clues.

#1 Who mourned deeply when he thought Joseph was dead?

JOBAC

#2 What nickname did Joseph's brothers give him?

REMEDAR

#3 Who was captain of the Egyptian palace guard?

TOPPIHRA

#4 What is a crafty plan called?

MECSHE

#5 Who convinced his brothers not to kill Joseph?

EBENRU

MYSTERY QUESTION:
Arrange the circled letters to answer the mystery question.

Who helped sell his brother into slavery?

THE CASE OF THE BIG ESCAPE

EXODUS 2:11-25

Unscramble the Jumbles, one letter to each space, to spell words as suggested by the trivia clues.

#1 What's another word for "murdered"?

DLELKI

#2 When something makes you feel far from home, what is it?

RNOGIFE

#3 Who was Moses' son?

MERGHOS

#4 What do you call people who take care of sheep?

PHRESHEDS

#5 What is another word for "forced servitude"?

VALSYER

MYSTERY QUESTION:
Arrange the circled letters to answer the mystery question.

Where did Moses escape to?

103

THE CASE OF
THE TEN PUNISHMENTS

EXODUS 7:14–10:29

Unscramble the Jumbles, one letter to each space, to spell words as suggested by the trivia clues.

#1 What are jumping amphibians called?

GRFSO

#2 What are man-made waterways?

LASANC

#3 What's a synonym for "prophesied"?

DRIDTEPEC

#4 What are large groups of insects called?

MRSSAW

#5 What is the opposite of "accept"?

SEERUF

MYSTERY QUESTION:
Arrange the circled letters to answer the mystery question.

How did God punish Pharaoh and the Egyptians for their hard-heartedness?

THE CASE OF
THE AMAZING ESCAPE

EXODUS 11–13

Unscramble the Jumbles, one letter to each space, to spell words as suggested by the trivia clues.

#1 What was an Egyptian king called?

HHORAAP

#2 What is another name for "nation"?

NOTRUCY

#3 What Jewish holiday marked the event when God saved the Israelites from the final plague?

SOPASEVR

#4 What is the oldest child in a family called?

TROFBRINS

#5 At what time did God say he would pass through Egypt?

NIDGIMHT

MYSTERY QUESTION:
Arrange the circled letters to answer the mystery question.

What country did Moses lead the Israelites out of?

THE CASE OF THE MIRACULOUS CROSSING

EXODUS 14:15-31

Unscramble the Jumbles, one letter to each space, to spell words as suggested by the trivia clues.

#1 What are edges or walls called?

SSEDI

#2 What chariot parts became a problem for Pharaoh's army?

LEHESW

#3 What is one of the ways God led the Israelites?

ULOCD

#4 Who enslaved the Israelites?

NYGSEAITP

#5 What are those who operated ancient horse-drawn vehicles called?

ROHEECIRSAT

MYSTERY QUESTION:
Arrange the circled letters to answer the mystery question.

What did the Israelites cross to get to safety?

THE CASE OF THE FURIOUS KING

MATTHEW 2:13-18

Unscramble the Jumbles, one letter to each space, to spell words as suggested by the trivia clues.

#1 Which prophet predicted that there would be great mourning in Israel?

MERJEHIA

#2 What's another word for "crying"?

PENWEGI

#3 What's another word for "cruel"?

RLATUB

#4 What are girls and boys?

NELDHIRC

#5 What evil king was in power when Jesus was born?

DROEH

MYSTERY QUESTION:
Arrange the circled letters to answer the mystery question.

In what town were young boys murdered because of the king's fury?

107

THE CASE OF THE AMAZING MESSAGE

MATTHEW 3:1-17

Unscramble the Jumbles, one letter to each space, to spell words as suggested by the trivia clues.

#1 What is an outward sign of faith that uses water?

BATMISP

#2 Which prophet predicted that John the Baptist would come?

ASIHAI

#3 What's another way to say "carries along"?

GRSNBI

#4 What is another word for "needs"?

SREERIQU

#5 What is the sound made by your vocal cords?

CIOVE

MYSTERY QUESTION:
Arrange the circled letters to answer the mystery question.

Where did the voice come from at Jesus' baptism?

108

THE CASE OF
THE SURPRISED PIGS
MATTHEW 8:28-34

Unscramble the Jumbles, one letter to each space, to spell words as suggested by the trivia clues.

#1 Who takes care of groups of animals?

MEERSDNH

#2 What is a synonym for "forceful"?

LEVITON

#3 How would you describe a hill with a sharp incline?

TEPES

#4 What is another way to say "fell quickly"?

GLENUPD

#5 What is a burial ground?

MEETRYEC

MYSTERY QUESTION:
Arrange the circled letters to answer the mystery question.

What did Jesus cast into the pigs?

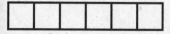

THE CASE OF THE TWELVE-YEAR TROUBLE

MATTHEW 9:20-22

Unscramble the Jumbles, one letter to each space, to spell words as suggested by the trivia clues.

#1 What is a brief period of time?

NOMMTE

#2 What is another word for "belief"?

TIFHA

#3 What is a synonym for "ongoing"?

ANNTTCOS

#4 What is another word for "healthy"?

LEWL

#5 What is the edge of a robe called?

NIRFEG

MYSTERY QUESTION:
Arrange the circled letters to answer the mystery question.

What ill person did Jesus heal?

110

THE CASE OF THE MIGHTY MIRACLES
MATTHEW 12:22-37

Unscramble the Jumbles, one letter to each space, to spell words as suggested by the trivia clues.

#1 What's another way to say "stands against"?

POSSOPE

#2 What is it called when someone is quarreling or arguing?

NIUDEFG

#3 What did Jesus do for many sick people?

EEHLDA

#4 What's another name for "earth"?

LROWD

#5 What does someone do when they judge or criticize another person?

MONNDEC

MYSTERY QUESTION:
Arrange the circled letters to answer the mystery question.

What did Jesus' miracles show him to be?

THE CASE OF PETER'S AMAZING REVELATION

MATTHEW 16:13-20

Unscramble the Jumbles, one letter to each space, to spell words as suggested by the trivia clues.

#1 If you won't allow something, what's another word for that?

BROFID

#2 What is the opposite of "take"?

VIEG

#3 What do you use to unlock doors?

SEKY

#4 What was Peter's given name?

MOINS

#5 Where did Jesus say his father was?

VAHNEE

MYSTERY QUESTION:
Arrange the circled letters to answer the mystery question.

What did Jesus give Peter the keys to?

THE CASE OF THE TRAITOROUS FRIEND

MATTHEW 26:47-56

Unscramble the Jumbles, one letter to each space, to spell words as suggested by the trivia clues.

#1 What do you call someone who betrays another person?

RTORTAI

#2 What wooden weapons are also one of the four suits in a deck of cards?

BLSUC

#3 What's another word for "snatched"?

DREBBAG

#4 Who was betrayed by one of his followers?

ESJUS

#5 What are sharp-edged weapons?

DRSWOS

MYSTERY QUESTION:
Arrange the circled letters to answer the mystery question.

Which disciple betrayed Jesus?

THE CASE OF
THE DESTROYED DRAPE
MATTHEW 27:45-56

Unscramble the Jumbles, one letter to each space, to spell words as suggested by the trivia clues.

#1 What was the holy place in the Temple called?

YUCANSTAR

#2 What are burial caves called?

BOMTS

#3 What is at fault when the earth shakes?

KERTAQUHAE

#4 What is another word for "really"?

LTYUR

#5 What is another way to say "torn in half"?

STILP

MYSTERY QUESTION:
Arrange the circled letters to answer the mystery question.

In the Temple, what tore at the moment of Jesus' death?

THE CASE OF
THE SICK MOTHER-IN-LAW
MARK 1:29-34

Unscramble the Jumbles, one letter to each space, to spell words as suggested by the trivia clues.

#1 Who was Simon's brother?

W R A D N E

#2 What is the opposite of "before"?

F R A E T

#3 What's another way to say "many different"?

S R U V A O I

#4 If you aided someone, what did you do?

P L E E D H

#5 What are evil spirits called?

N O M E D S

MYSTERY QUESTION:
Arrange the circled letters to answer the mystery question.

What was Simon's mother-in-law's illness?

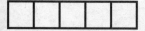

115

THE CASE OF
JESUS' TRUE IDENTITY

MARK 8:22-30

Unscramble the Jumbles, one letter to each space, to spell words as suggested by the trivia clues.

#1 Which Old Testament prophet was Jesus compared to?

> JILHEA

#2 If you are getting saliva out of your mouth, what are you doing?

> TIPSGINT

#3 What do you call the place you live?

> MOHE

#4 What part of the face comes in different colors?

> YSEE

#5 What is it called when you put your hands on something?

> CUTOH

MYSTERY QUESTION:
Arrange the circled letters to answer the mystery question.

Who did Peter say Jesus was?

THE CASE OF THE FORCEFUL FAITH

MARK 9:14-29

Unscramble the Jumbles, one letter to each space, to spell words as suggested by the trivia clues.

#1 What do you call the earth beneath your feet?

URGDON

#2 What is another word for "unbelieving"?

SLEFATSIH

#3 What is a synonym for "forcefully"?

LIONTVYEL

#4 What do you use to eat?

TUMOH

#5 When is "right away"?

TTLAINYSN

MYSTERY QUESTION:
Arrange the circled letters to answer the mystery question.

What is possible if a person believes?

117

THE CASE OF THE MISSING BOY

LUKE 2:41-52

Unscramble the Jumbles, one letter to each space, to spell words as suggested by the trivia clues.

#1 What's another word for "celebration"?

LEVITASF

#2 How many is a dozen?

VEELWT

#3 Who are people on a journey?

RRAEETSVL

#4 Whose parents were searching for him?

USSJE

#5 What were you if you were awestruck?

MAADEZ

MYSTERY QUESTION:
Arrange the circled letters to answer the mystery question.

Where was the Temple Jesus visited as a child?

THE CASE OF THE WEEPING WIDOW

LUKE 7:11-17

Unscramble the Jumbles, one letter to each space, to spell words as suggested by the trivia clues.

#1 What is a burial box?

FOFCNI

#2 Who is a female parent?

RETMHO

#3 What is the opposite of old?

GUNYO

#4 What is another name for a small town?

ALIVLEG

#5 What are casket carriers called?

REERABS

MYSTERY QUESTION:
Arrange the circled letters to answer the mystery question.

At what event did Jesus raise a boy from the dead?

THE CASE OF BREAD FROM HEAVEN

JOHN 6:30-35

Unscramble the Jumbles, one letter to each space, to spell words as suggested by the trivia clues.

#1 What are you if you crave water?

TSTRIYH

#2 What is the opposite of "take"?

VEGI

#3 What did the Israelites eat in the wilderness?

NANAM

#4 If something happens that only God could do, how might you describe it?

CRAIMOSULU

#5 What is the opposite of "false"?

RETU

MYSTERY QUESTION:
Arrange the circled letters to answer the mystery question.

What will people who come to Jesus never be?

THE CASE OF THE DISBELIEVING DISCIPLE

JOHN 20:24-29

Unscramble the Jumbles, one letter to each space, to spell words as suggested by the trivia clues.

#1 What are injuries to the body called?

DUWSON

#2 What didn't stop Jesus from entering the room, even though they were locked?

ODROS

#3 What is another word for "cried out"?

MALIDEXEC

#4 How many original disciples were there?

VELWET

#5 What word would describe someone who doesn't believe?

SLATIFHES

MYSTERY QUESTION:
Arrange the circled letters to answer the mystery question.

Who was the disbelieving disciple?

121

THE CASE OF THE VERY LONG NIGHT
JOHN 21:1-25

Unscramble the Jumbles, one letter to each space, to spell words as suggested by the trivia clues.

#1   What is the place where the water meets the land?

ROSEH

#2   What is your morning meal?

FAAREKTBS

#3   What is another word for "worship"?

RILFGYO

#4   What was Peter's outer garment called?

NUICT

#5   Who was one of Jesus' followers from Cana?

TAANNLEHA

MYSTERY QUESTION:
Arrange the circled letters to answer the mystery question.

What were the disciples doing when Jesus appeared?

THE CASE OF
THE DRAMATIC ROAD TRIP
ACTS 9:1-19

Unscramble the Jumbles, one letter to each space, to spell words as suggested by the trivia clues.

#1 What fell from Paul's eyes?

```
C L A S S E
[ ][ ][ ][ ][(○)][ ]
```

#2 What is the street that the Lord sent Ananias to?

```
T R T I H S G A
[ ][(○)][ ][ ][ ][ ][ ][ ]
```

#3 If a person is picked, what is he or she?

```
S O C N H E
[ ][ ][ ][ ][(○)][ ]
```

#4 What might your enemy keep doing to you?

```
N I C E S E P R T U G
[ ][(○)][ ][(○)][ ][ ][ ][ ][ ][ ][ ]
```

#5 What direction do you go when you fall off a horse?

```
N D W O
[(○)][ ][(○)][ ]
```

MYSTERY QUESTION:
Arrange the circled letters to answer the mystery question.

What did the Lord do to Saul's life?

```
[ ][ ][ ][ ][ ][ ][ ]
```

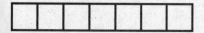

123

THE CASE OF THE NEW MISSIONARY PARTNER

ACTS 15:22–19:10

Unscramble the Jumbles, one letter to each space, to spell words as suggested by the trivia clues.

#1 What is a town Paul visited in Syria?

COANHIT

#2 What are people called who belong to a certain city or group of people?

NICETIZS

#3 What was an island Paul visited?

PRYCSU

#4 How did Paul travel over water?

DEAILS

#5 What is it called when two things have come together?

DEONJI

MYSTERY QUESTION:
Arrange the circled letters to answer the mystery question.

Who was added to Paul's ministry team?

THE CASE OF
THE PREACHING PARTNER
1 TIMOTHY 1–2

Unscramble the Jumbles, one letter to each space, to spell words as suggested by the trivia clues.

#1 Where did Paul urge his spiritual son to remain?

SEESHUP

#2 What are directions to be followed?

SNITOSNICTUR

#3 What is it called when you praise God for who he is?

WIPHORS

#4 What term for an early disciple means "one who is sent"?

STOPALE

#5 What is another word for "grace"?

CRYME

MYSTERY QUESTION:
Arrange the circled letters to answer the mystery question.

Who was Paul's friend and spiritual son?

125

GOD MAKES THE WORLD
GENESIS 1–2

Unscramble the Jumbles and put them into their corresponding spaces in the Criss-Cross puzzle. Then unscramble the circled letters to find the mystery answer.

ACROSS

2	Nickname for large-toothed aquatic animals	**G T R S O A**
6	Our planet	**H R E T A**
7	Elegant swimming birds	**W S N A S**

DOWN

1	Area set aside for plants	**D R N A G E**
3	Fire on a stick	**C T R H O**
4	Existence	**E I F L**
5	Animals with feathers	**B I S D R**

MYSTERY ANSWER:

Arrange the circled letters to solve the mystery answer.

God said his _____ was good.

☐ ☐ ☐ ☐ ☐ ☐ ☐ ☐ ☐

126

TWO EVIL CITIES

GENESIS 19:1-29

Unscramble the Jumbles and put them into their corresponding spaces in the Criss-Cross puzzle.
Then unscramble the circled letters to find the mystery answer.

ACROSS

3	Making light of a situation	KJOGIN
4	Reasonable; sensible	OLAGLCI
7	Anxious; excited	AEERG

DOWN

1	Small town	ILAVEGL
2	Pillar	NULCMO
5	To move around sneakily	PEECR
6	Rush	UYHRR

MYSTERY ANSWER:
Arrange the circled letters to solve the mystery answer.

God destroyed the sinful cities of Sodom and _____.

EXTREME OBEDIENCE

GENESIS 22

Unscramble the Jumbles and put them into their corresponding spaces in the Criss-Cross puzzle. Then unscramble the circled letters to find the mystery answer.

ACROSS

1	Kitchen tool with a blade	NEKIF
5	Captured	CUGTAH
7	Son or daughter	IHLCD
8	Not closer	FRTERAH

DOWN

2	Son of Abraham	SICAA
3	Type of breakfast muffin	GLNEHSI
4	Cast a ballot	TODVE
6	Steep edge of a mountain	FLICF

MYSTERY ANSWER:

Arrange the circled letters to solve the mystery answer.

God told Abraham to _____ his son.

☐☐☐☐☐☐☐☐☐☐

A STRUGGLE WITH GOD

GENESIS 32:22-32

Unscramble the Jumbles and put them into their corresponding spaces in the Criss-Cross puzzle. Then unscramble the circled letters to find the mystery answer.

ACROSS

#	Clue	Jumble
1	Married females	WVEIS
4	Wound; damage to the body	YNIUJR
5	Path or street	NEAL
6	Arose from sleep	KOWE
7	Type of competition	HACTM

DOWN

#	Clue	Jumble
2	Pay no attention to	NEGIOR
3	Hired helper	NETSRAV

MYSTERY ANSWER:

Arrange the circled letters to solve the mystery answer.

An angel came to Jacob's camp to _____ with him.

☐ ☐ ☐ ☐ ☐ ☐ ☐

THE BUSH THAT DIDN'T BURN UP

EXODUS 3–4

Unscramble the Jumbles and put them into their corresponding spaces in the Criss-Cross puzzle. Then unscramble the circled letters to find the mystery answer.

ACROSS

1 Scare — RGFTEHIN

3 God's Word — EBILB

5 Earth's surface — RNGUDO

6 Written down or captured on audio — EDCREDRO

DOWN

1 Flame — EFRI

2 Early nighttime — NVEEGIN

4 Noise — UDONS

MYSTERY ANSWER:

Arrange the circled letters to solve the mystery answer.

The bush Moses saw didn't burn up even though it was _____ in flames.

☐☐☐☐☐☐☐☐

A YEARLY CELEBRATION

EXODUS 11–12

*Unscramble the Jumbles and put them into their corresponding spaces in the Criss-Cross puzzle.
Then unscramble the circled letters to find the mystery answer.*

ACROSS

1	Before second	IFTRS
2	Baby sheep	AMLB
6	Houses	SMEOH
7	Likes	NEJSOY

DOWN

1	Grand meal	ESFTA
3	In need of lots of bandages	ODOBLY
4	Cats have nine	EVISL
5	Opposite of "humility"	RDIEP

MYSTERY ANSWER:
Arrange the circled letters to solve the mystery answer.

The Israelites celebrated the _____ feast.

☐☐☐☐☐☐☐☐

THE ISRAELITES DISOBEY
EXODUS 32

*Unscramble the Jumbles and put them into their corresponding spaces in the Criss-Cross puzzle.
Then unscramble the circled letters to find the mystery answer.*

ACROSS

2 Baby cow **ACFL**

5 Piece of jewelry **IRARENG**

6 Made an art project with clay **EODLMD**

DOWN

1 Proposal **FOERF**

3 Rage **GRENA**

4 Twisted **UTDNRE**

MYSTERY ANSWER:
Arrange the circled letters to solve the mystery answer.

The Israelites made a false God in the form of a _____ calf.

JUMBLE CRISS-CROSS #8
A TALKING ANIMAL
NUMBERS 22:21-41

Unscramble the Jumbles and put them into their corresponding spaces in the Criss-Cross puzzle.
Then unscramble the circled letters to find the mystery answer.

ACROSS

1 Shoreline   **TOCAS**

4 An ill wish spoken against someone   **URECS**

6 Irritate   **YONAN**

DOWN

2 To talk   **PAKSE**

3 Sharp weapon   **WRSOD**

5 Unlace   **NUTEI**

MYSTERY ANSWER:
Arrange the circled letters to solve the mystery answer.

God gave Balaam's _____ the ability to speak to him.

133

AS CLOSE AS BROTHERS
1 SAMUEL 18; 20; 23

*Unscramble the Jumbles and put them into their corresponding spaces in the Criss-Cross puzzle.
Then unscramble the circled letters to find the mystery answer.*

ACROSS

3 Not here — HETER

4 Turning the wheel of a vehicle — EREGITSN

6 Riddles — EJSKO

DOWN

1 Pals — IERDFNS

2 Keeping out of sight — HNGIDI

4 Long, pointed weapon — EASRP

5 Fences — AGSTE

MYSTERY ANSWER:

Arrange the circled letters to solve the mystery answer.

David's best buddy was _____.

134

SEVEN DIPS IN THE RIVER

2 KINGS 5:1-19

Unscramble the Jumbles and put them into their corresponding spaces in the Criss-Cross puzzle. Then unscramble the circled letters to find the mystery answer.

ACROSS

3 Servant's boss

4 Finds similarities

A S E T R M

R E A S O M C P

DOWN

1 Nine minus two

2 Receive a gift

5 Stubborn animals

6 One more time

E N S V E

C T E A C P

L M U S E

N G I A A

MYSTERY ANSWER:

Arrange the circled letters to solve the mystery answer.

Elisha healed _____ of leprosy.

135

SADNESS OVER A CITY

NEHEMIAH 1:1-11

Unscramble the Jumbles and put them into their corresponding spaces in the Criss-Cross puzzle. Then unscramble the circled letters to find the mystery answer.

ACROSS

1	Feeling of wrongdoing	HSMAE
6	Illness	CKSISNSE
7	High respect	ORHNO

DOWN

2	How tall something is	IGTHEH
3	Creating	GAMINK
4	Clenched hands	TISSF
5	Scared feeling	EFAR

MYSTERY ANSWER:

Arrange the circled letters to solve the mystery answer.

_____ was the king's cup-bearer.

A PROPHET WITH A TOUGH JOB

JEREMIAH 8:18–9:2

*Unscramble the Jumbles and put them into their corresponding spaces in the Criss-Cross puzzle.
Then unscramble the circled letters to find the mystery answer.*

ACROSS

1 To discipline or penalize   IUPHSN

5 Cries   IASLW

6 Bring back to the original state   SERERTO

7 Silly   FOGOY

DOWN

2 Sounds   ONIESS

3 Unnamed person   DSBYEOMO

4 One who forms clay   POETRT

MYSTERY ANSWER:
Arrange the circled letters to solve the mystery answer.

Jeremiah was the _____ prophet.

A NIGHT WITH THE LIONS

DANIEL 6

Unscramble the Jumbles and put them into their corresponding spaces in the Criss-Cross puzzle. Then unscramble the circled letters to find the mystery answer.

ACROSS

1 Wonder Woman and Supergirl   EIHNSERO

4 The king of the Medes and Persians   AISDUR

5 Spoke to God   AYPRDE

DOWN

1 The part of a suitcase used to carry it   NDAHEL

2 Policeman   COEIRFF

3 Baby's room   RUERYSN

MYSTERY ANSWER:

Arrange the circled letters to solve the mystery answer.

_____ kept praying to God, even though he knew he'd be punished for it.

A VISION IN THE NIGHT
MATTHEW 1:18-25

*Unscramble the Jumbles and put them into their corresponding spaces in the Criss-Cross puzzle.
Then unscramble the circled letters to find the mystery answer.*

ACROSS

1 Old Testament king who was Solomon's father   **VIADD**

4 In front of everyone   **BCLPUI**

6 Total   **CTELOMPE**

7 Occur   **EHNPPA**

DOWN

2 Noise level   **OVUELM**

3 Most recent   **ENSETW**

5 Something untold   **CSRETE**

MYSTERY ANSWER:
Arrange the circled letters to solve the mystery answer.

An angel _____ to Joseph in a dream.

HEALING ON THE LORD'S DAY

MATTHEW 12:9-14

Unscramble the Jumbles and put them into their corresponding spaces in the Criss-Cross puzzle. Then unscramble the circled letters to find the mystery answer.

ACROSS

2	Brag	**TOABS**
5	Body part at the end of an arm	**DNHA**
6	Performed surgery	**PREDETAO**

DOWN

1	Vision	**TSGIH**
2	Take along	**RBIGN**
3	Academic topics	**SETJBUCS**
4	Listened	**HDARE**

MYSTERY ANSWER:

Arrange the circled letters to solve the mystery answer.

Jesus healed a man's crippled hand on the _____.

JESUS ON TRIAL

MATTHEW 27:11-26

Unscramble the Jumbles and put them into their corresponding spaces in the Criss-Cross puzzle. Then unscramble the circled letters to find the mystery answer.

ACROSS

2 Person behind bars — EPRSINRO

4 To depart — EAELV

5 What you use to wipe your face — KPANIN

DOWN

1 End of life on earth — DHETA

2 Pilate's home — APLECA

3 To form an idea of — GEMAINI

MYSTERY ANSWER:

Arrange the circled letters to solve the mystery answer.

The crowd told Pilate to _____ Barabbas, the criminal.

⬚⬚⬚⬚⬚⬚⬚

141

JESUS' FINAL INSTRUCTIONS

MATTHEW 28:16-20

Unscramble the Jumbles and put them into their corresponding spaces in the Criss-Cross puzzle. Then unscramble the circled letters to find the mystery answer.

ACROSS

1 Cost — RIEPC

5 Five plus six — VELEEN

7 Kenyan or Sudanese — FCIARNA

8 Most secure — SEFTSA

DOWN

2 Four-leafed symbol of luck — ROLEVC

3 Instruction; order — AOMMNCD

4 Opposite of "never" — AYWASL

6 Parts of the body under the chin — KESCN

MYSTERY ANSWER:

Arrange the circled letters to solve the mystery answer.

Jesus said, "Go and make _____ of all the nations."

☐ ☐ ☐ ☐ ☐ ☐ ☐ ☐ ☐

THROUGH THE ROOF
MARK 2:1-12

Unscramble the Jumbles and put them into their corresponding spaces in the Criss-Cross puzzle.
Then unscramble the circled letters to find the mystery answer.

ACROSS

1 Take from one place to another   **R A C Y R**

5 Opening   **O H L E**

7 Big ocean wave   **L I T D A**

8 Quickly   **I A R Y P L D**

DOWN

2 Ceiling of a house   **F T P O R O O**

3 Give way; surrender   **L E D I Y**

4 At last   **A L F Y I N L**

6 Rips   **S E A T R**

MYSTERY ANSWER:
Arrange the circled letters to solve the mystery answer.

Jesus healed a _____ who was lowered from the ceiling.

BACK TO LIFE!

MARK 5:21-43

*Unscramble the Jumbles and put them into their corresponding spaces in the Criss-Cross puzzle.
Then unscramble the circled letters to find the mystery answer.*

ACROSS

1	Ocean robber	TPAIER
5	Specific pattern for doing something	DORER
6	Citrus fruit	GRAEON
7	Complete; detailed	TRHOHOGU

DOWN

1	Old Testament messenger of God	PTPOERH
2	Music player	DOARI
3	Funnel storm	ROTDAON
4	Suitcases	GULGGAE

MYSTERY ANSWER:

Arrange the circled letters to solve the mystery answer.

Jesus healed Jairus's _____.

AN INCREDIBLE ANNOUNCEMENT

LUKE 1

*Unscramble the Jumbles and put them into their corresponding spaces in the Criss-Cross puzzle.
Then unscramble the circled letters to find the mystery answer.*

ACROSS

1 Use your mind   **KHINT**

4 Strength or might   **RPEWO**

5 Heavenly being   **LGEAN**

DOWN

1 Extreme fear   **RTRREO**

2 Young infant   **BONWENR**

3 Month of showers   **PAIRL**

MYSTERY ANSWER:

Arrange the circled letters to solve the mystery answer.

_____ told Mary she would be Jesus' mother.

☐ ☐ ☐ ☐ ☐ ☐ ☐

TWO SISTERS HAVE COMPANY

LUKE 10:38-42

Unscramble the Jumbles and put them into their corresponding spaces in the Criss-Cross puzzle. Then unscramble the circled letters to find the mystery answer.

ACROSS

1 Specifics   I E L D T S A

4 A quick peek   E P L S M G I

5 Object   G I T N H

DOWN

1 Small weapon similar to a knife   E G A D R G

2 Dryness in the mouth   R T S T H I

3 Hear   S L N E I T

MYSTERY ANSWER:

Arrange the circled letters to solve the mystery answer.

Mary's sister, _____, was distracted by all the work that needed to be done.

GOD SEES THE HEART

LUKE 18:9-14

Unscramble the Jumbles and put them into their corresponding spaces in the Criss-Cross puzzle.
Then unscramble the circled letters to find the mystery answer.

ACROSS

1	Opposite of "day"	GHITN
4	Lots	NAMY
6	Words spoken to God	REYRAP
7	Extreme sadness	ROWSOR

DOWN

2	Not proud	BLUMHE
3	Place where the Jews worshiped	PLEMTE
5	Expresses gratitude	KHANTS

MYSTERY ANSWER:
Arrange the circled letters to solve the mystery answer.

The _____ thought he was better than the tax collector.

☐☐☐☐☐☐☐☐☐

FAREWELL . . . FOR NOW
LUKE 24:35-53

Unscramble the Jumbles and put them into their corresponding spaces in the Criss-Cross puzzle. Then unscramble the circled letters to find the mystery answer.

ACROSS

1 Feel with your hand   **UCOTH**

3 To come into sight   **RAPAPE**

6 Truthful   **TEOSNH**

7 Frighten or surprise   **ARTSTEL**

DOWN

2 Needed right away   **GENTUR**

4 Get up   **SIRE**

5 To pursue   **SAHEC**

MYSTERY ANSWER:

Arrange the circled letters to solve the mystery answer.

Jesus was lifted to heaven during his _____.

FAITHFUL TO THE END
ACTS 6:8–7:60

Unscramble the Jumbles and put them into their corresponding spaces in the Criss-Cross puzzle.
Then unscramble the circled letters to find the mystery answer.

ACROSS

1	One who is killed for his or her beliefs	**A M R T R Y**
4	Stones	**C O S K R**
7	Ending a career	**E N T I R G R I**

DOWN

2	Take into police custody	**R E A R T S**
3	An answer	**E S S R O N E P**
5	To go forward at full speed	**H R E C A G**
6	Challenges	**S E A D R**

MYSTERY ANSWER:
Arrange the circled letters to solve the mystery answer.

_____ was stoned to death for his faith.

☐☐☐☐☐☐☐

149

MONEY CAN'T BUY GOD'S POWER

ACTS 8:9-25

Unscramble the Jumbles and put them into their corresponding spaces in the Criss-Cross puzzle. Then unscramble the circled letters to find the mystery answer.

ACROSS

1	Let others use what you have	**EASHR**
5	Buy	**ARPUCSEH**
6	Energizing; full of anticipation	**ITEGIXCN**
7	In the middle of	**MAGNO**

DOWN

1	Basic	**EMILPS**
2	Response	**IEROCNAT**
3	Might; power	**GTHNRSTE**
4	Sorcery	**GMCAI**

MYSTERY ANSWER:

Arrange the circled letters to solve the mystery answer.

Simon from Samaria was once a _____.

DISASTER AND DELIVERANCE

GENESIS 7–9

Use the clues to help unscramble the Jumbles, one letter to each space, to spell words that relate to this Scripture passage.

#1 LOOFD   CLUE: Water disaster

#2 TRFYO   CLUE: Fifty minus ten

#3 GRINEVOC   CLUE: Wrapping

#4 RURCSY   CLUE: Scamper

#5 ODSRTEY   CLUE: Ruin

Find and circle the answers (from above) in the grid of letters below.

U	E	N	X	C	M	J	B	J	G	O	Y	Y	U
D	J	J	K	P	B	T	F	N	S	P	R	X	B
E	B	U	E	Z	J	Z	I	T	T	R	O	W	Z
S	H	J	F	F	B	R	T	Q	U	K	C	J	C
T	C	S	X	L	E	U	T	C	K	G	S	L	K
R	K	M	M	V	O	C	S	F	I	O	B	N	T
O	Q	S	O	Y	Z	O	F	O	R	T	Y	R	C
Y	U	C	E	B	U	P	D	W	A	T	J	Z	O

TWO BROTHERS MAKE PEACE
GENESIS 32–33

Use the clues to help unscramble the Jumbles, one letter to each space, to spell words that relate to this Scripture passage.

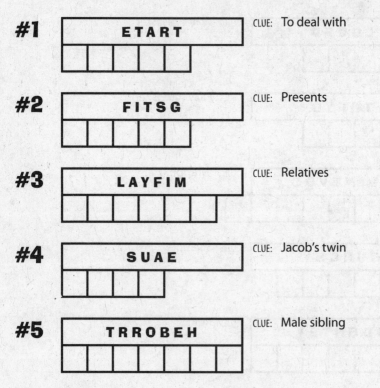

#1 `E T A R T`

CLUE: To deal with

#2 `F I T S G`

CLUE: Presents

#3 `L A Y F I M`

CLUE: Relatives

#4 `S U A E`

CLUE: Jacob's twin

#5 `T R R O B E H`

CLUE: Male sibling

Find and circle the answers (from above) in the grid of letters below.

G	N	U	E	S	A	U	P	I	Z	D	Q	F	H
W	I	Z	O	C	C	C	T	R	Y	Q	Q	R	B
J	R	F	J	Q	F	O	Y	T	R	M	K	E	E
F	U	L	T	I	C	L	A	R	W	Y	G	V	B
B	J	X	F	S	I	E	Z	J	W	E	F	R	H
B	G	Y	D	M	R	B	R	O	T	H	E	R	E
Q	D	X	A	T	P	E	A	C	E	P	U	F	D
F	M	F	X	V	P	Q	G	U	T	M	B	D	R

PHARAOH'S NIGHTMARES

GENESIS 41:1-36

Use the clues to help unscramble the Jumbles, one letter to each space, to spell words that relate to this Scripture passage.

#1 | S R G S A | CLUE: Cow chow

#2 | N A G R I | CLUE: What bread or cereal is made of

#3 | C I M I A A G N S | CLUE: Illusionists

#4 | M E F N I A | CLUE: Severe shortage of food

#5 | S O R P P T Y I E R | CLUE: Wealth; success

Find and circle the answers (from above) in the grid of letters below.

P	R	O	S	P	E	R	I	T	Y	G	N	O	N
L	F	F	O	G	X	G	O	S	J	R	A	F	H
W	V	A	R	Q	D	W	S	Q	P	E	G	Z	N
H	C	C	M	O	R	A	G	I	G	Q	J	K	Q
D	J	U	U	I	R	I	P	R	U	C	C	U	J
M	B	T	B	G	N	T	P	T	A	N	Z	V	S
J	K	B	N	D	T	E	Y	B	Q	I	Y	J	Y
Z	G	M	A	G	I	C	I	A	N	S	N	B	Q

TOUGH TIMES IN EGYPT
EXODUS 5:6-23

Use the clues to help unscramble the Jumbles, one letter to each space, to spell words that relate to this Scripture passage.

#1 PLPYSU

CLUE: Provide

#2 CRBISK

CLUE: Blocks used to build a house

#3 RSIREDV

CLUE: Those who get things and people to move

#4 REPOUDC

CLUE: Manufacture

#5 NIKTS

CLUE: To smell bad

Find and circle the answers (from above) in the grid of letters below.

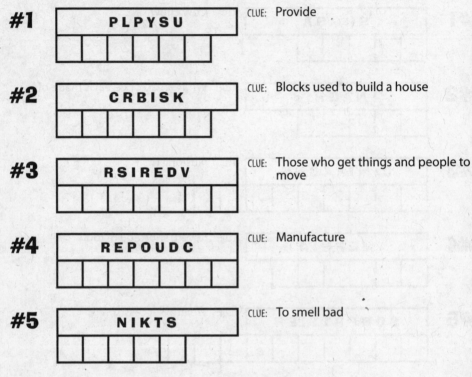

Q	Z	E	Y	U	X	V	P	H	N	Y	Y	F	Y
F	Q	B	W	T	G	S	R	Y	H	L	V	U	H
S	E	O	R	B	K	T	O	A	P	Q	Z	U	K
I	T	G	A	C	N	I	D	P	A	H	K	A	H
Q	K	I	I	H	W	E	U	X	E	T	F	M	R
V	J	R	N	R	K	S	C	R	Q	Z	B	E	D
B	B	R	E	K	P	J	E	A	B	S	S	U	L
L	Y	D	R	I	V	E	R	S	R	Z	N	L	V

RAHAB TO THE RESCUE
JOSHUA 2

Use the clues to help unscramble the Jumbles, one letter to each space, to spell words that relate to this Scripture passage.

#1 | S S E I P | CLUE: Secret watchers

#2 | O C E M | CLUE: Move toward

#3 | N E D I D H | CLUE: Out of sight

#4 | C U S T O | CLUE: To explore or investigate

#5 | O W W N I D | CLUE: Opening in the wall

Find and circle the answers (from above) in the grid of letters below.

N	Y	A	X	T	G	F	V	T	A	S	E	B	J
B	O	C	U	S	Y	I	N	C	M	H	I	E	Z
V	W	O	B	H	W	K	L	G	M	F	M	K	Q
D	C	I	S	P	I	E	S	Q	S	O	R	F	E
S	P	I	N	N	O	D	E	A	C	R	K	S	Y
N	U	S	N	D	W	V	D	L	U	C	K	S	C
Q	A	K	V	A	O	W	E	E	L	M	T	S	P
Y	V	A	Q	Z	O	W	X	G	N	Z	P	Y	O

TRUSTING GOD IN TOUGH TIMES

JOB 3–11; 42

Use the clues to help unscramble the Jumbles, one letter to each space, to spell words that relate to this Scripture passage.

#1 G R U S E L G T

CLUE: Situation filled with difficulty

#2 R E M I S Y

CLUE: Complete sadness or suffering

#3 T E R N E P

CLUE: To turn away from sin

#4 C E S U J I T

CLUE: Fairness

#5 N I N E O N C C E

CLUE: Freedom from guilt

Find and circle the answers (from above) in the grid of letters below.

I	N	N	O	C	E	N	C	E	I	Q	Y	E	P
U	G	J	U	S	T	I	C	E	Z	R	L	M	D
P	C	Z	M	N	Q	N	X	H	E	G	Y	P	C
Z	C	K	E	K	Y	J	X	S	G	M	Z	V	M
V	C	P	K	T	A	T	I	U	E	G	N	B	F
N	E	F	K	J	N	M	R	J	H	Y	R	H	T
R	B	V	J	K	L	T	J	F	Z	R	L	N	D
E	I	L	L	S	T	A	J	N	J	M	J	O

GOD KNOWS YOU, INSIDE AND OUT

PSALM 139

Use the clues to help unscramble the Jumbles, one letter to each space, to spell words that relate to this Scripture passage.

#1 THARE
CLUE: Part of your body that pumps blood

#2 NEESECRP
CLUE: Opposite of "absence"

#3 LOOLFW
CLUE: Go behind a leader

#4 XIDMEENA
CLUE: Inspected or looked closely at

#5 HOTTHUGS
CLUE: Mental processes

Find and circle the answers (from above) in the grid of letters below.

L	E	G	U	U	A	T	T	M	Y	B	A	D	Q
X	X	G	R	J	R	P	H	J	C	O	V	I	I
F	A	J	T	F	T	O	O	L	P	I	V	E	S
O	M	M	K	E	D	B	U	I	M	C	P	Q	Z
L	I	R	D	P	Y	C	G	N	W	A	F	U	E
L	N	F	X	J	R	F	H	M	C	D	S	M	Z
O	E	C	H	E	A	R	T	A	N	T	Z	M	O
W	D	S	Y	P	R	E	S	E	N	C	E	W	N

WORDS OF WISDOM
PROVERBS 1–4

Use the clues to help unscramble the Jumbles, one letter to each space, to spell words that relate to this Scripture passage.

#1 SOOFL CLUE: People who aren't wise

#2 RHOON CLUE: Esteem; respect

#3 IDWEKC CLUE: Evil

#4 SEWI CLUE: Full of insight

#5 CCISEHO CLUE: Decisions

Find and circle the answers (from above) in the grid of letters below.

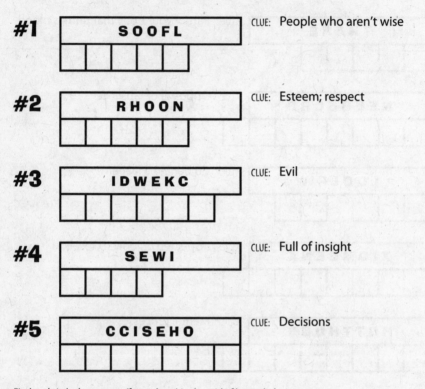

Y	F	F	D	M	W	I	C	K	E	D	F	B	L
V	C	O	N	O	E	J	D	D	O	B	J	S	T
Q	G	O	V	W	S	O	X	R	M	K	B	J	A
H	H	L	C	I	Q	V	T	D	F	J	Y	S	M
H	O	S	G	S	A	I	X	K	S	D	H	L	W
Q	H	N	W	E	Y	J	Q	X	D	G	N	J	Z
C	W	Q	O	U	A	C	H	O	I	C	E	S	X
X	Q	K	Q	R	N	T	W	K	A	I	A	F	S

A TIME FOR EVERYTHING

ECCLESIASTES 3

Use the clues to help unscramble the Jumbles, one letter to each space, to spell words that relate to this Scripture passage.

#1 R N I A G S E H C   CLUE: Looking for

#2 D R U N E B   CLUE: Heavy weight

#3 A N O S S E   CLUE: Fall, winter, spring, or summer

#4 T U U F E R   CLUE: Time to come

#5 N O S T E S   CLUE: Small rocks

Find and circle the answers (from above) in the grid of letters below.

R	H	D	M	R	E	Y	V	R	D	D	X	U	J
W	Z	W	G	R	H	Z	V	F	F	N	O	E	B
G	W	U	U	S	V	F	M	V	K	W	T	P	B
X	F	T	C	B	E	F	B	U	R	D	E	N	Y
R	U	L	W	S	E	A	R	C	H	I	N	G	O
F	C	S	T	O	N	E	S	L	J	Q	Z	P	H
W	X	X	H	R	V	Z	R	O	C	O	Y	I	C
A	Q	G	T	G	L	N	Q	V	N	O	Y	R	D

THE WRITING ON THE WALL

DANIEL 5

Use the clues to help unscramble the Jumbles, one letter to each space, to spell words that relate to this Scripture passage.

#1 NAHD CLUE: Part of the body with five fingers

#2 SLEBNO CLUE: Respected members of society

#3 LAEP CLUE: White in the face

#4 DULMEHB CLUE: Brought low; not proud

#5 UPLERP CLUE: Royal color

Find and circle the answers (from above) in the grid of letters below.

F	Q	U	K	V	U	A	E	A	S	G	P	R	W
D	P	V	A	W	N	L	J	E	A	E	T	K	E
V	P	A	R	B	P	V	L	H	C	A	F	F	W
D	P	E	L	R	H	B	C	A	U	A	W	A	O
H	F	M	U	E	O	G	Z	P	V	W	Q	D	Q
A	N	P	N	N	N	H	U	M	B	L	E	D	D
N	S	I	O	Y	W	U	U	Q	F	E	D	S	S
D	T	S	U	K	O	Q	C	J	G	M	Z	T	R

A FAMOUS SERMON

MATTHEW 6:5-18

Use the clues to help unscramble the Jumbles, one letter to each space, to spell words that relate to this Scripture passage.

#1 | M T E P T | CLUE: To lead into sin

#2 | G R O F E V I | CLUE: To pardon sins

#3 | V E E N A H | CLUE: God's dwelling

#4 | D E B A R | CLUE: Sandwich material

#5 | L O H Y | CLUE: Sacred

Find and circle the answers (from above) in the grid of letters below.

P	Y	J	K	M	H	I	D	V	D	Y	Y	D	B
D	E	Y	N	O	X	E	H	A	L	L	O	W	R
H	U	N	Z	E	U	U	A	O	G	O	Q	E	E
X	K	B	V	O	B	C	H	V	V	Z	T	R	A
I	K	K	D	H	T	D	T	C	E	P	U	U	D
A	H	Y	L	F	A	E	T	T	M	N	N	J	S
F	O	R	G	I	V	E	U	E	P	Y	Z	X	Z
N	K	Q	E	L	V	C	T	J	S	E	T	P	X

WALKING ON WATER
MARK 6:45-56

Use the clues to help unscramble the Jumbles, one letter to each space, to spell words that relate to this Scripture passage.

#1 THOGS

CLUE: Eerie, shadowy figure

#2 GRWONI

CLUE: Using oars

#3 RTDWOA

CLUE: In the direction of

#4 SORESIU

CLUE: Not joking

#5 GEARUCO

CLUE: Bravery

Find and circle the answers (from above) in the grid of letters below.

E	X	U	R	D	V	D	C	R	F	S	T	O	F
E	Z	E	O	H	R	S	G	E	G	N	B	I	G
J	K	M	L	A	L	L	E	U	I	B	S	T	L
L	R	F	W	C	A	Q	L	R	A	G	N	Y	V
G	H	O	S	T	Q	U	K	L	I	C	N	G	G
Z	T	C	O	U	R	A	G	E	R	O	Q	V	G
M	K	H	E	R	O	W	I	N	G	A	U	Z	G
O	R	Y	B	Q	Y	U	Q	W	W	V	D	S	J

LITTLE BECOMES MUCH

MARK 8:1-10

Use the clues to help unscramble the Jumbles, one letter to each space, to spell words that relate to this Scripture passage.

#1 OBTA
CLUE: Water transportation

#2 GEHUNO
CLUE: Plenty

#3 TADEWN
CLUE: Desired

#4 DEPKIC
CLUE: Gathered; chose

#5 KROBE
CLUE: Ripped apart

Find and circle the answers (from above) in the grid of letters below.

I	D	P	I	C	K	E	D	Y	H	K	T	U	L
Q	Y	K	L	O	K	C	T	W	C	Q	Q	G	P
P	A	T	N	O	I	X	N	H	I	M	N	G	O
Q	V	K	R	A	Y	K	A	Z	O	T	Y	B	Y
J	G	B	R	B	H	O	P	D	S	I	B	J	H
A	F	X	V	X	O	T	G	W	U	I	I	L	F
S	C	E	Z	S	W	A	W	A	N	T	E	D	H
E	N	O	U	G	H	B	T	I	P	D	Z	D	S

163

CLEARING THE TEMPLE

MARK 11:15-18

Use the clues to help unscramble the Jumbles, one letter to each space, to spell words that relate to this Scripture passage.

#1   S E V O D   CLUE: Peaceful white birds

#2   S E E H I T V   CLUE: Robbers

#3   G U N Y I B   CLUE: Purchasing

#4   D E R T U N   CLUE: Transformed

#5   S E H U O   CLUE: Home

Find and circle the answers (from above) in the grid of letters below.

G	G	V	W	O	B	U	Y	I	N	G	W	K	A
G	M	D	R	Z	E	Q	X	O	L	X	D	U	E
H	F	C	A	S	T	H	I	E	V	E	S	X	C
D	Z	D	U	R	Q	C	X	E	N	U	X	I	C
A	K	O	O	S	I	S	I	R	Y	O	B	L	V
B	H	W	C	V	R	Q	U	S	G	M	J	T	E
D	N	A	Y	U	E	T	Y	O	F	V	B	V	U
Z	V	O	B	U	I	S	O	K	M	I	K	Y	R

JESUS IS PUT IN THE GRAVE

MARK 15:42-47

Use the clues to help unscramble the Jumbles, one letter to each space, to spell words that relate to this Scripture passage.

#1 DRAFYI
CLUE: Final weekday

#2 SEJHOP
CLUE: The man who helped bury Jesus' body

#3 NINEL
CLUE: Cloth often used for bedsheets

#4 NOTSE
CLUE: Large rock

#5 TANNECER
CLUE: Opposite of "exit"

Find and circle the answers (from above) in the grid of letters below.

```
O J Z F R I D A Y E T U S A
X N O P C G G U C H N Z V L
S C A Q L Q L N P A E U W A
O C O B U P A E L N H B Q L
U H R P G R S K O K H Q E L
A M F K T O S T M P U D U O
V H J N J N S L I N E N Y L
R A E T R K T G R H V Y Z P
```

THE BEST NEWS
MARK 16:1-11

Use the clues to help unscramble the Jumbles, one letter to each space, to spell words that relate to this Scripture passage.

#1 N K O I O L G CLUE: Searching

#2 B T M O CLUE: Grave

#3 V E E N N G I CLUE: Sundown

#4 R A L B I U CLUE: Ceremony following death

#5 T E E R N D E CLUE: Opposite of "exited"

Find and circle the answers (from above) in the grid of letters below.

W	B	E	A	Z	P	L	E	N	K	H	L	X	T
O	E	V	N	L	K	A	C	G	L	B	N	W	G
Z	U	E	W	T	J	G	N	A	N	G	Y	K	N
P	E	N	E	F	E	I	I	K	K	B	M	D	S
G	H	I	W	Z	K	R	R	Y	M	K	Z	D	S
T	V	N	I	O	U	R	E	O	W	Q	S	U	G
S	W	G	O	B	T	Z	T	D	M	J	S	K	I
K	K	L	L	T	L	P	Z	O	K	O	O	U	T

GOOD NEWS OF GREAT JOY

LUKE 2:8-20

Use the clues to help unscramble the Jumbles, one letter to each space, to spell words that relate to this Scripture passage.

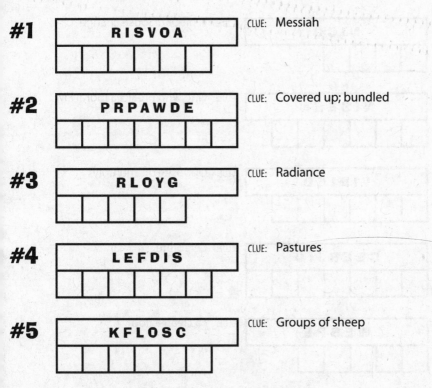

#1   RISVOA   CLUE: Messiah

#2   PRPAWDE   CLUE: Covered up; bundled

#3   RLOYG   CLUE: Radiance

#4   LEFDIS   CLUE: Pastures

#5   KFLOSC   CLUE: Groups of sheep

Find and circle the answers (from above) in the grid of letters below.

F	G	T	A	Q	Y	V	O	M	Z	Q	Z	C	Q
K	T	S	Z	R	F	S	F	Q	N	J	Z	D	U
F	A	I	O	S	Z	B	F	L	O	C	K	S	F
W	I	L	W	R	A	P	P	E	D	N	G	P	G
K	G	E	W	D	C	V	Z	T	S	X	K	D	F
G	J	D	L	O	O	F	I	N	T	B	G	V	I
C	L	C	Z	D	V	P	X	O	T	S	G	E	A
F	H	L	G	P	S	A	T	P	R	K	Z	K	T

LOST AND FOUND
LUKE 15

Use the clues to help unscramble the Jumbles, one letter to each space, to spell words that relate to this Scripture passage.

#1   NICO

CLUE: A piece of loose change

#2   NISERN

CLUE: One who breaks a moral law

#3   VIDIED

CLUE: Opposite of "multiply"

#4   CEERJIO

CLUE: Celebrate

#5   WESPE

CLUE: To clean a floor

Find and circle the answers (from above) in the grid of letters below.

D	E	O	N	I	C	B	U	X	F	X	W	L	W
I	F	A	L	O	O	S	T	J	C	Z	N	F	J
V	S	W	J	S	I	L	I	Z	B	I	D	A	L
I	D	W	D	W	N	S	R	E	J	O	I	C	E
D	K	X	U	E	N	D	R	L	R	N	C	L	Z
E	T	K	O	E	Y	P	R	N	O	L	N	Q	S
H	T	U	A	P	U	K	Q	H	T	M	K	F	A
X	X	P	C	S	I	N	N	E	R	E	W	L	F

FIND THE JUMBLE #19

MIRACLE AT A WEDDING
JOHN 2:1-12

Use the clues to help unscramble the Jumbles, one letter to each space, to spell words that relate to this Scripture passage.

#1 N I W E

CLUE: Strong drink made from grapes

#2 K R N I D

CLUE: To consume a liquid

#3 D W E D G N I

CLUE: Marriage celebration

#4 V A N T S S R E

CLUE: Hired help

#5 L O L A N S G

CLUE: Measurements for milk and other liquids

Find and circle the answers (from above) in the grid of letters below.

W	E	D	D	I	N	G	A	Z	L	J	A	U	B
D	H	M	R	Y	X	L	W	D	M	Q	L	H	D
R	G	D	D	X	Z	T	K	D	M	F	Z	P	A
I	O	D	I	Z	W	S	E	R	V	A	N	T	S
N	Z	L	Z	K	I	U	P	E	T	F	Y	I	K
K	G	F	W	J	N	R	U	P	B	M	A	V	L
A	X	Q	B	M	E	A	G	A	L	L	O	N	S
D	C	V	E	P	A	D	M	H	M	B	K	R	C

169

THE LIGHT GOD SENT TO EARTH

JOHN 8:12-20

Use the clues to help unscramble the Jumbles, one letter to each space, to spell words that relate to this Scripture passage.

#1 TLGHI

L i g h t

CLUE: Illumination

#2 HARFET

CLUE: Parent

#3 MEOC

CLUE: To move toward

#4 SESNAKRD

CLUE: Opposite of "light"

#5 NUGTJMED

CLUE: Punishment

Find and circle the answers (from above) in the grid of letters below.

J	F	E	O	D	W	F	C	O	M	E	O	R	D
U	I	L	I	G	H	T	W	F	K	L	K	A	J
D	O	F	J	W	K	D	A	R	K	N	E	S	S
G	E	N	K	K	Y	D	E	Z	D	I	H	O	B
M	U	K	A	B	T	H	O	D	V	B	F	Q	N
E	M	X	X	N	T	E	H	S	K	F	E	W	B
N	O	E	P	A	Y	U	E	U	U	F	S	G	W
T	X	K	F	H	H	U	T	U	W	M	B	F	N

170

SHIPWRECK!
ACTS 27:27-44

Use the clues to help unscramble the Jumbles, one letter to each space, to spell words that relate to this Scripture passage.

#1

| M R S T O |

CLUE: Heavy rain

#2

| R A A D I F |

CLUE: Scared

#3

| N A N W D I G |

CLUE: Breaking of day

#4

| L R S S I O A |

CLUE: The crew of a ship

#5

| A O G R C |

CLUE: Freight

Find and circle the answers (from above) in the grid of letters below.

W	B	R	Z	R	D	A	W	N	I	N	G	J	Z
E	X	Y	Y	O	E	B	G	X	S	A	D	D	P
T	Z	Q	G	E	M	P	S	O	E	I	E	C	B
S	W	R	B	A	X	Y	T	P	A	T	U	J	G
I	A	K	D	W	S	T	O	R	M	E	D	L	T
C	W	E	Z	J	O	F	F	Q	I	M	R	O	H
A	G	J	E	H	S	A	I	L	O	R	S	A	Y
Y	R	J	R	G	W	H	H	K	A	U	I	I	M

WHAT LOVE LOOKS LIKE
1 CORINTHIANS 13

Use the clues to help unscramble the Jumbles, one letter to each space, to spell words that relate to this Scripture passage.

#1 TTIPENA   CLUE: Willing to put up with a lot

#2 SGVIE   CLUE: Opposite of "takes"

#3 VRROEEF   CLUE: Never-ending

#4 REESNUD   CLUE: Lasts; withstands

#5 NIGEDA   CLUE: Acquired

Find and circle the answers (from above) in the grid of letters below.

D	Z	Z	N	R	B	J	T	G	S	Z	W	G	Q
K	Z	H	R	K	Y	P	D	O	W	N	I	D	K
L	I	L	O	G	X	J	A	U	T	X	E	T	A
N	U	F	B	U	I	C	D	T	W	N	S	O	L
F	G	F	O	R	E	V	E	R	I	N	U	C	A
K	C	B	V	V	A	U	E	A	C	E	V	M	Q
R	X	S	Z	B	T	Q	G	S	Q	B	N	R	T
E	N	D	U	R	E	S	J	G	A	S	A	T	K

GOD'S ARMOR

EPHESIANS 6:10-20

Use the clues to help unscramble the Jumbles, one letter to each space, to spell words that relate to this Scripture passage.

#1 YNEEM

CLUE: A hostile person or force

#2 MORRA

A r m o r

CLUE: Protective body wear

#3 LEHSDI

S h e i l d

CLUE: Something you hold up to protect yourself

#4 TLEEMH

H e l m e t

CLUE: Headgear

#5 SWORAR

CLUE: Bow's partners

Find and circle the answers (from above) in the grid of letters below.

N	Q	B	V	A	A	Z	O	B	O	J	P	D	H
T	L	K	V	I	S	H	I	E	L	D	K	J	B
F	A	Y	F	Y	B	E	L	A	E	W	L	G	Z
I	X	R	M	I	Y	L	A	Y	B	H	H	M	U
E	D	E	R	A	H	M	N	R	O	L	R	O	G
N	N	K	A	O	O	E	M	Z	M	D	K	A	S
E	W	J	W	R	W	T	Z	D	E	O	D	V	A
U	S	R	C	T	O	S	K	I	W	Z	R	W	D

173

THE KIND OF FAITH THAT PLEASES GOD

JAMES 1–3

Use the clues to help unscramble the Jumbles, one letter to each space, to spell words that relate to this Scripture passage.

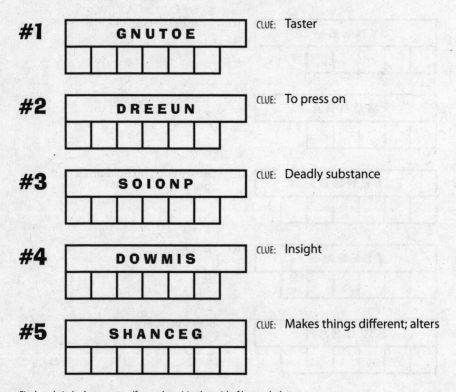

#1 GNUTOE CLUE: Taster

#2 DREEUN CLUE: To press on

#3 SOIONP CLUE: Deadly substance

#4 DOWMIS CLUE: Insight

#5 SHANCEG CLUE: Makes things different; alters

Find and circle the answers (from above) in the grid of letters below.

Y	R	F	Z	G	T	E	P	D	U	U	S	K	X
Y	V	F	B	N	R	I	I	K	T	E	E	C	W
E	N	D	U	R	E	G	C	E	G	U	L	H	I
A	R	P	G	U	E	I	G	N	G	G	M	Z	S
W	N	C	B	U	T	Y	A	N	C	P	O	G	D
Z	V	A	U	M	N	H	O	K	W	H	C	D	O
X	X	L	K	H	C	T	L	A	D	T	O	C	M
R	G	W	N	Q	W	P	O	I	S	O	N	T	R

A VISION OF HEAVEN

REVELATION 1, 20–22

Use the clues to help unscramble the Jumbles, one letter to each space, to spell words that relate to this Scripture passage.

#1 HECCUHRS CLUE: Places of worship

#2 ICTEIS CLUE: Big towns

#3 OLSUS CLUE: The spirits of people

#4 DIZESE CLUE: Took hold of

#5 GRONDA CLUE: Fire-breathing creature

Find and circle the answers (from above) in the grid of letters below.

L	K	D	C	D	Z	C	I	T	I	E	S	J	J
W	V	C	H	F	C	Z	T	T	W	E	M	N	V
C	Q	Z	U	G	P	R	M	S	E	I	Z	E	D
M	P	U	R	D	O	O	L	T	N	J	P	C	G
Z	V	E	C	H	J	U	Y	J	T	U	B	K	G
A	V	E	H	P	O	X	C	L	P	K	V	K	R
E	X	W	E	S	R	D	R	A	G	O	N	M	X
K	P	G	S	E	Y	R	N	U	O	U	G	A	H

THE CALL OF ABRAM

GENESIS 12:1-9

See if you can unscramble the mixed-up letters to make the words without looking at the passage first. If you get stumped, look for the answers in the verses below.

#1 SLENBIGS

#2 ORNAHTE

#3 RAALT

#4 NLDA

#5 VINTAE

#6 USNCITETDR

The LORD had said to Abram, "Leave your native country, your relatives, and your father's family, and go to the land that I will show you. I will make you into a great nation. I will bless you and make you famous, and you will be a blessing to others. I will bless those who bless you and curse those who treat you with contempt. All the families on earth will be blessed through you." So Abram departed as the LORD had instructed, and Lot went with him. Abram was seventy-five years old when he left Haran. He took his wife, Sarai, his nephew Lot, and all his wealth—his livestock and all the people he had taken into his household at Haran—and headed for the land of Canaan. When they arrived in Canaan, Abram traveled through the land as far as Shechem. There he set up camp beside the oak of Moreh. At that time, the area was inhabited by Canaanites. Then the LORD appeared to Abram and said, "I will give this land to your descendants." And Abram built an altar there and dedicated it to the LORD, who had appeared to him. After that, Abram traveled south and set up camp in the hill country, with Bethel to the west and Ai to the east. There he built another altar and dedicated it to the LORD, and he worshiped the LORD. Then Abram continued traveling south by stages toward the Negev.

GENESIS 12:1-9

MYSTERY ANSWER:

THE BIRTH OF ISAAC

GENESIS 21:1-7

See if you can unscramble the mixed-up letters to make the words without looking at the passage first. If you get stumped, look for the answers in the verses below.

#1 LREEDADC

#2 TIHEG

#3 RESUN

#4 LAXTECY

#5 NROB

#6 MEEBAC

The Lᴏʀᴅ kept his word and did for Sarah exactly what he had promised. She became pregnant, and she gave birth to a son for Abraham in his old age. This happened at just the time God had said it would. And Abraham named their son Isaac. Eight days after Isaac was born, Abraham circumcised him as God had commanded. Abraham was 100 years old when Isaac was born. And Sarah declared, "God has brought me laughter. All who hear about this will laugh with me. Who would have said to Abraham that Sarah would nurse a baby? Yet I have given Abraham a son in his old age!"

GENESIS 21:1-7

MYSTERY ANSWER:

THE SCOUTING REPORT
NUMBERS 13:25-33

See if you can unscramble the mixed-up letters to make the words without looking at the passage first. If you get stumped, look for the answers in the verses below.

#1 DOTOS

#2 VORUED

#3 REEFOB

#4 RONUCYT

#5 NLVIGI

#6 TAANIGS

After exploring the land for forty days, the men returned to Moses, Aaron, and the whole community of Israel at Kadesh in the wilderness of Paran. They reported to the whole community what they had seen and showed them the fruit they had taken from the land. This was their report to Moses: "We entered the land you sent us to explore, and it is indeed a bountiful country—a land flowing with milk and honey. Here is the kind of fruit it produces. But the people living there are powerful, and their towns are large and fortified. We even saw giants there, the descendants of Anak! The Amalekites live in the Negev, and the Hittites, Jebusites, and Amorites live in the hill country. The Canaanites live along the coast of the Mediterranean Sea and along the Jordan Valley." But Caleb tried to quiet the people as they stood before Moses. "Let's go at once to take the land," he said. "We can certainly conquer it!" But the other men who had explored the land with him disagreed. "We can't go up against them! They are stronger than we are!" So they spread this bad report about the land among the Israelites: "The land we traveled through and explored will devour anyone who goes to live there. All the people we saw were huge. We even saw giants there, the descendants of Anak. Next to them we felt like grasshoppers, and that's what they thought, too!"

NUMBERS 13:25-33

MYSTERY ANSWER:

JONAH'S PRAYER

JONAH 2:1-10

See if you can unscramble the mixed-up letters to make the words without looking at the passage first. If you get stumped, look for the answers in the verses below.

#1 WRTHE

#2 SCBAK

#3 CRIEEMS

#4 SPEDTH

#5 GYTMIH

#6 NEVRID

Then Jonah prayed to the LORD his God from inside the fish. He said, "I cried out to the LORD in my great trouble, and he answered me. I called to you from the land of the dead, and LORD, you heard me! You threw me into the ocean depths, and I sank down to the heart of the sea. The mighty waters engulfed me; I was buried beneath your wild and stormy waves. Then I said, 'O LORD, you have driven me from your presence. Yet I will look once more toward your holy Temple.' I sank beneath the waves, and the waters closed over me. Seaweed wrapped itself around my head. I sank down to the very roots of the mountains. I was imprisoned in the earth, whose gates lock shut forever. But you, O LORD my God, snatched me from the jaws of death! As my life was slipping away, I remembered the LORD. And my earnest prayer went out to you in your holy Temple. Those who worship false Gods turn their backs on all God's mercies. But I will offer sacrifices to you with songs of praise, and I will fulfill all my vows. For my salvation comes from the LORD alone." Then the LORD ordered the fish to spit Jonah out onto the beach.

JONAH 2:1-10

MYSTERY ANSWER:

JESUS' TEMPTATION
MATTHEW 4:1-11

See if you can unscramble the mixed-up letters to make the words without looking at the passage first. If you get stumped, look for the answers in the verses below.

#1 GHIH

#2 DOSWHE

#3 RGUIDN

#4 KPAE

#5 LNEAO

#6 TENOS

Then Jesus was led by the Spirit into the wilderness to be tempted there by the devil. For forty days and forty nights he fasted and became very hungry. During that time the devil came and said to him, "If you are the Son of God, tell these stones to become loaves of bread." But Jesus told him, "No! The Scriptures say, 'People do not live by bread alone, but by every word that comes from the mouth of God.'" Then the devil took him to the holy city, Jerusalem, to the highest point of the Temple, and said, "If you are the Son of God, jump off! For the Scriptures say, 'He will order his angels to protect you. And they will hold you up with their hands so you won't even hurt your foot on a stone.'" Jesus responded, "The Scriptures also say, 'You must not test the LORD your God.'" Next the devil took him to the peak of a very high mountain and showed him all the kingdoms of the world and their glory. "I will give it all to you," he said, "if you will kneel down and worship me." "Get out of here, Satan," Jesus told him. "For the Scriptures say, 'You must worship the LORD your God and serve only him.'" Then the devil went away, and angels came and took care of Jesus.

MATTHEW 4:1-11

MYSTERY ANSWER:

SERMON ON THE MOUNT
MATTHEW 5:3-12

See if you can unscramble the mixed-up letters to make the words without looking at the passage first. If you get stumped, look for the answers in the verses below.

#1 STREIH

#2 LGDA

#3 SLBSESE

#4 BLUMHE

#5 TOBAU

#6 ZELAEIR

"God blesses those who are poor and realize their need for him, for the Kingdom of Heaven is theirs. God blesses those who mourn, for they will be comforted. God blesses those who are humble, for they will inherit the whole earth. God blesses those who hunger and thirst for justice, for they will be satisfied. God blesses those who are merciful, for they will be shown mercy. God blesses those whose hearts are pure, for they will see God. God blesses those who work for peace, for they will be called the children of God. God blesses those who are persecuted for doing right, for the Kingdom of Heaven is theirs. God blesses you when people mock you and persecute you and lie about you and say all sorts of evil things against you because you are my followers. Be happy about it! Be very glad! For a great reward awaits you in heaven. And remember, the ancient prophets were persecuted in the same way."

MATTHEW 5:3-12

MYSTERY ANSWER:

COUNTING THE COST
MATTHEW 8:18-22

See if you can unscramble the mixed-up letters to make the words without looking at the passage first. If you get stumped, look for the answers in the verses below.

#1 SILERIUOG

#2 SOFXE

#3 EPCLA

#4 DROL

#5 REEVRHEW

#6 NORUDA

When Jesus saw the crowd around him, he instructed his disciples to cross to the other side of the lake. Then one of the teachers of religious law said to him, "Teacher, I will follow you wherever you go." But Jesus replied, "Foxes have dens to live in, and birds have nests, but the Son of Man has no place even to lay his head." Another of his disciples said, "Lord, first let me return home and bury my father." But Jesus told him, "Follow me now. Let the spiritually dead bury their own dead."

MATTHEW 8:18-22

MYSTERY ANSWER:

182

JESUS CALMS THE STORM
MATTHEW 8:23-27

See if you can unscramble the mixed-up letters to make the words without looking at the passage first. If you get stumped, look for the answers in the verses below.

#1 RONDW

#2 NRABGEKI

#3 SNDIW

#4 LUNDSDYE

#5 BYEO

Then Jesus got into the boat and started across the lake with his disciples. Suddenly, a fierce storm struck the lake, with waves breaking into the boat. But Jesus was sleeping. The disciples went and woke him up, shouting, "Lord, save us! We're going to drown!" Jesus responded, "Why are you afraid? You have so little faith!" Then he got up and rebuked the wind and waves, and suddenly there was a great calm. The disciples were amazed. "Who is this man?" they asked. "Even the winds and waves obey him!"

MATTHEW 8:23-27

MYSTERY ANSWER:

JESUS HEALS THE BLIND

MATTHEW 9:27-31

See if you can unscramble the mixed-up letters to make the words without looking at the passage first. If you get stumped, look for the answers in the verses below.

#1 EMKA

#2 MAFE

#3 DLBNI

#4 PEHNAP

#5 VADDI

#6 NIBEDH

After Jesus left the girl's home, two blind men followed along behind him, shouting, "Son of David, have mercy on us!" They went right into the house where he was staying, and Jesus asked them, "Do you believe I can make you see?" "Yes, Lord," they told him, "we do." Then he touched their eyes and said, "Because of your faith, it will happen." Then their eyes were opened, and they could see! Jesus sternly warned them, "Don't tell anyone about this." But instead, they went out and spread his fame all over the region.

MATTHEW 9:27-31

MYSTERY ANSWER:

JESUS VS. A DEMON

MATTHEW 9:32-34

See if you can unscramble the mixed-up letters to make the words without looking at the passage first. If you get stumped, look for the answers in the verses below.

#1 M D O E N

D e m o n

#2 T R O B U G H

#3 S E E B A C U

#4 H I N T O N G

#5 D L I M E X E A C

#6 S O P S E E D S S

When they left, a demon-possessed man who couldn't speak was brought to Jesus. So Jesus cast out the demon, and then the man began to speak. The crowds were amazed. "Nothing like this has ever happened in Israel!" they exclaimed. But the Pharisees said, "He can cast out demons because he is empowered by the prince of demons."

MATTHEW 9:32-34

MYSTERY ANSWER:

185

JESUS ENTERS JERUSALEM
MATTHEW 21:1-11

See if you can unscramble the mixed-up letters to make the words without looking at the passage first. If you get stumped, look for the answers in the verses below.

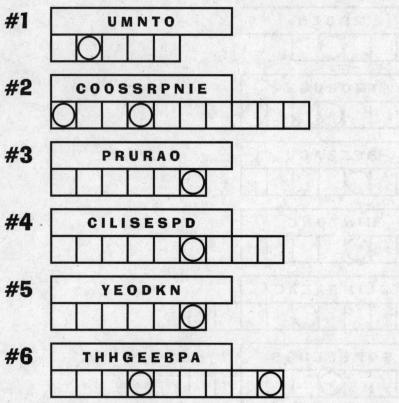

#1 UMNTO

#2 COOSSRPNIE

#3 PRURAO

#4 CILISESPD

#5 YEODKN

#6 THHGEEBPA

As Jesus and the disciples approached Jerusalem, they came to the town of Bethphage on the Mount of Olives. Jesus sent two of them on ahead. "Go into the village over there," he said. "As soon as you enter it, you will see a donkey tied there, with its colt beside it. Untie them and bring them to me. If anyone asks what you are doing, just say, 'The Lord needs them,' and he will immediately let you take them." This took place to fulfill the prophecy that said, "Tell the people of Jerusalem, 'Look, your King is coming to you. He is humble, riding on a donkey—riding on a donkey's colt.'" The two disciples did as Jesus commanded. They brought the donkey and the colt to him and threw their garments over the colt, and he sat on it. Most of the crowd spread their garments on the road ahead of him, and others cut branches from the trees and spread them on the road. Jesus was in the center of the procession, and the people all around him were shouting, "Praise God for the Son of David! Blessings on the one who comes in the name of the LORD! Praise God in highest heaven!" The entire city of Jerusalem was in an uproar as he entered. "Who is this?" they asked. And the crowds replied, "It's Jesus, the prophet from Nazareth in Galilee."

MATTHEW 21:1-11

MYSTERY ANSWER:

JESUS IN GETHSEMANE

MATTHEW 26:36-46

See if you can unscramble the mixed-up letters to make the words without looking at the passage first. If you get stumped, look for the answers in the verses below.

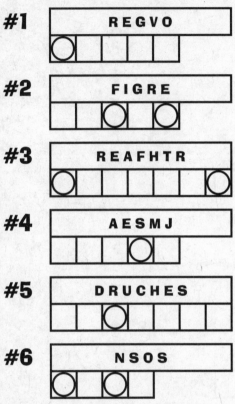

#1 REGVO

#2 FIGRE

#3 REAFHTR

#4 AESMJ

#5 DRUCHES

#6 NSOS

Then Jesus went with them to the olive grove called Gethsemane, and he said, "Sit here while I go over there to pray." He took Peter and Zebedee's two sons, James and John, and he became anguished and distressed. He told them, "My soul is crushed with grief to the point of death. Stay here and keep watch with me." He went on a little farther and bowed with his face to the ground, praying, "My Father! If it is possible, let this cup of suffering be taken away from me. Yet I want your will to be done, not mine." Then he returned to the disciples and found them asleep. He said to Peter, "Couldn't you watch with me even one hour? Keep watch and pray, so that you will not give in to temptation. For the spirit is willing, but the body is weak!" Then Jesus left them a second time and prayed, "My Father! If this cup cannot be taken away unless I drink it, your will be done." When he returned to them again, he found them sleeping, for they couldn't keep their eyes open. So he went to pray a third time, saying the same things again. Then he came to the disciples and said, "Go ahead and sleep. Have your rest. But look—the time has come. The Son of Man is betrayed into the hands of sinners. Up, let's be going. Look, my betrayer is here!"

MATTHEW 26:36-46

MYSTERY ANSWER:

PETER DENIES JESUS
MATTHEW 26:69-75

See if you can unscramble the mixed-up letters to make the words without looking at the passage first. If you get stumped, look for the answers in the verses below.

#1 SCWOR

#2 THAO

#3 LRITTYBE

#4 DLAFESH

#5 RNFOT

#6 RHANZAET

Meanwhile, Peter was sitting outside in the courtyard. A servant girl came over and said to him, "You were one of those with Jesus the Galilean." But Peter denied it in front of everyone. "I don't know what you're talking about," he said. Later, out by the gate, another servant girl noticed him and said to those standing around, "This man was with Jesus of Nazareth." Again Peter denied it, this time with an oath. "I don't even know the man," he said. A little later some of the other bystanders came over to Peter and said, "You must be one of them; we can tell by your Galilean accent." Peter swore, "A curse on me if I'm lying—I don't know the man!" And immediately the rooster crowed. Suddenly, Jesus' words flashed through Peter's mind: "Before the rooster crows, you will deny three times that you even know me." And he went away, weeping bitterly.

MATTHEW 26:69-75

MYSTERY ANSWER:

JOHN'S BIRTH
LUKE 1:57-66

See if you can unscramble the mixed-up letters to make the words without looking at the passage first. If you get stumped, look for the answers in the verses below.

#1 REVY

#2 TIRINGW

#3 RYLUSE

#4 FEELERTCD

#5 KEDAS

#6 NEEPADPH

When it was time for Elizabeth's baby to be born, she gave birth to a son. And when her neighbors and relatives heard that the Lord had been very merciful to her, everyone rejoiced with her. When the baby was eight days old, they all came for the circumcision ceremony. They wanted to name him Zechariah, after his father. But Elizabeth said, "No! His name is John!" "What?" they exclaimed. "There is no one in all your family by that name." So they used gestures to ask the baby's father what he wanted to name him. He motioned for a writing tablet, and to everyone's surprise he wrote, "His name is John." Instantly Zechariah could speak again, and he began praising God. Awe fell upon the whole neighborhood, and the news of what had happened spread throughout the Judean hills. Everyone who heard about it reflected on these events and asked, "What will this child turn out to be?" For the hand of the Lord was surely upon him in a special way.

LUKE 1:57-66

MYSTERY ANSWER:

189

THE BIRTH OF JESUS
LUKE 2:1-7

See if you can unscramble the mixed-up letters to make the words without looking at the passage first. If you get stumped, look for the answers in the verses below.

#1 LAAVIBEAL

#2 SLOOVIBYU

#3 EREGRSTI

#4 YUNSLG

#5 HOTLC

#6 MEOH

At that time the Roman emperor, Augustus, decreed that a census should be taken throughout the Roman Empire. (This was the first census taken when Quirinius was governor of Syria.) All returned to their own ancestral towns to register for this census. And because Joseph was a descendant of King David, he had to go to Bethlehem in Judea, David's ancient home. He traveled there from the village of Nazareth in Galilee. He took with him Mary, his fiancée, who was now obviously pregnant. And while they were there, the time came for her baby to be born. She gave birth to her first child, a son. She wrapped him snugly in strips of cloth and laid him in a manger, because there was no lodging available for them.

LUKE 2:1-7

MYSTERY ANSWER:

190

JESUS IN THE TEMPLE
LUKE 2:21-24

See if you can unscramble the mixed-up letters to make the words without looking at the passage first. If you get stumped, look for the answers in the verses below.

#1 ABYB

#2 NIVEG

#3 HNTE

#4 FREEDOF

#5 QERRIDEU

#6 VEEDICCON

Eight days later, when the baby was circumcised, he was named Jesus, the name given him by the angel even before he was conceived. Then it was time for their purification offering, as required by the law of Moses after the birth of a child; so his parents took him to Jerusalem to present him to the Lord. The law of the Lord says, "If a woman's first child is a boy, he must be dedicated to the LORD." So they offered the sacrifice required in the law of the Lord—"either a pair of turtledoves or two young pigeons."

LUKE 2:21-24

MYSTERY ANSWER:

THE FIRST DISCIPLES

LUKE 5:1-11

See if you can unscramble the mixed-up letters to make the words without looking at the passage first. If you get stumped, look for the answers in the verses below.

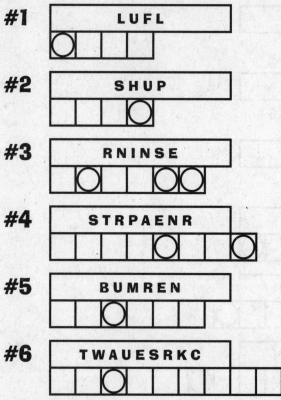

#1 LUFL

#2 SHUP

#3 RNINSE

#4 STRPAENR

#5 BUMREN

#6 TWAUESRKC

One day as Jesus was preaching on the shore of the Sea of Galilee, great crowds pressed in on him to listen to the word of God. He noticed two empty boats at the water's edge, for the fishermen had left them and were washing their nets. Stepping into one of the boats, Jesus asked Simon, its owner, to push it out into the water. So he sat in the boat and taught the crowds from there. When he had finished speaking, he said to Simon, "Now go out where it is deeper, and let down your nets to catch some fish." "Master," Simon replied, "we worked hard all last night and didn't catch a thing. But if you say so, I'll let the nets down again." And this time their nets were so full of fish they began to tear! A shout for help brought their partners in the other boat, and soon both boats were filled with fish and on the verge of sinking. When Simon Peter realized what had happened, he fell to his knees before Jesus and said, "Oh, Lord, please leave me—I'm too much of a sinner to be around you." For he was awestruck by the number of fish they had caught, as were the others with him. His partners, James and John, the sons of Zebedee, were also amazed. Jesus replied to Simon, "Don't be afraid! From now on you'll be fishing for people!" And as soon as they landed, they left everything and followed Jesus.

LUKE 5:1-11

MYSTERY ANSWER:

JESUS CURES LEPROSY

LUKE 5:12-16

See if you can unscramble the mixed-up letters to make the words without looking at the passage first. If you get stumped, look for the answers in the verses below.

#1 NYEOAN

#2 DEERCHA

#3 TIEDESP

#4 MANEEXI

#5 GLONA

#6 HIWTDWRE

In one of the villages, Jesus met a man with an advanced case of leprosy. When the man saw Jesus, he bowed with his face to the ground, begging to be healed. "Lord," he said, "if you are willing, you can heal me and make me clean." Jesus reached out and touched him. "I am willing," he said. "Be healed!" And instantly the leprosy disappeared. Then Jesus instructed him not to tell anyone what had happened. He said, "Go to the priest and let him examine you. Take along the offering required in the law of Moses for those who have been healed of leprosy. This will be a public testimony that you have been cleansed." But despite Jesus' instructions, the report of his power spread even faster, and vast crowds came to hear him preach and to be healed of their diseases. But Jesus often withdrew to the wilderness for prayer.

LUKE 5:12-16

MYSTERY ANSWER:

A ROMAN OFFICER'S FAITH

LUKE 7:1-10

See if you can unscramble the mixed-up letters to make the words without looking at the passage first. If you get stumped, look for the answers in the verses below.

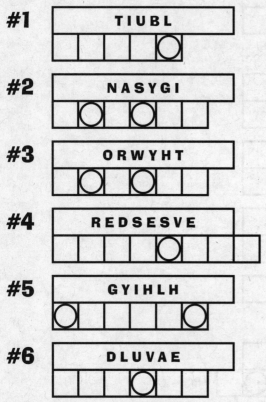

#1 TIUBL

#2 NASYGI

#3 ORWYHT

#4 REDSESVE

#5 GYIHLH

#6 DLUVAE

When Jesus had finished saying all this to the people, he returned to Capernaum. At that time the highly valued slave of a Roman officer was sick and near death. When the officer heard about Jesus, he sent some respected Jewish elders to ask him to come and heal his slave. So they earnestly begged Jesus to help the man. "If anyone deserves your help, he does," they said, "for he loves the Jewish people and even built a synagogue for us." So Jesus went with them. But just before they arrived at the house, the officer sent some friends to say, "Lord, don't trouble yourself by coming to my home, for I am not worthy of such an honor. I am not even worthy to come and meet you. Just say the word from where you are, and my servant will be healed.

I know this because I am under the authority of my superior officers, and I have authority over my soldiers. I only need to say, 'Go,' and they go, or 'Come,' and they come. And if I say to my slaves, 'Do this,' they do it." When Jesus heard this, he was amazed. Turning to the crowd that was following him, he said, "I tell you, I haven't seen faith like this in all Israel!" And when the officer's friends returned to his house, they found the slave completely healed.

LUKE 7:1-10

MYSTERY ANSWER:

194

JESUS FEEDS A CROWD

LUKE 9:10-17

See if you can unscramble the mixed-up letters to make the words without looking at the passage first. If you get stumped, look for the answers in the verses below.

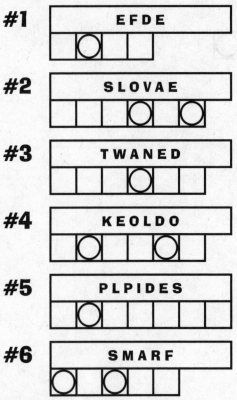

#1 EFDE

#2 SLOVAE

#3 TWANED

#4 KEOLDO

#5 PLPIDES

#6 SMARF

When the apostles returned, they told Jesus everything they had done. Then he slipped quietly away with them toward the town of Bethsaida. But the crowds found out where he was going, and they followed him. He welcomed them and taught them about the Kingdom of God, and he healed those who were sick. Late in the afternoon the twelve disciples came to him and said, "Send the crowds away to the nearby villages and farms, so they can find food and lodging for the night. There is nothing to eat here in this remote place." But Jesus said, "You feed them." "But we have only five loaves of bread and two fish," they answered. "Or are you expecting us to go and buy enough food for this whole crowd?" For there were about 5,000 men there. Jesus replied, "Tell them to sit down in groups of about fifty each." So the people all sat down. Jesus took the five loaves and two fish, looked up toward heaven, and blessed them. Then, breaking the loaves into pieces, he kept giving the bread and fish to the disciples so they could distribute it to the people. They all ate as much as they wanted, and afterward, the disciples picked up twelve baskets of leftovers!

LUKE 9:10-17

MYSTERY ANSWER:

GOD REVEALED

LUKE 9:28-36

See if you can unscramble the mixed-up letters to make the words without looking at the passage first. If you get stumped, look for the answers in the verses below.

#1 ZGADINLZ

#2 NLALEF

#3 ARPYNGI

#4 HTCESLO

#5 GPIPRDE

#6 RUDLEBT

About eight days later Jesus took Peter, John, and James up on a mountain to pray. And as he was praying, the appearance of his face was transformed, and his clothes became dazzling white. Suddenly, two men, Moses and Elijah, appeared and began talking with Jesus. They were glorious to see. And they were speaking about his exodus from this world, which was about to be fulfilled in Jerusalem. Peter and the others had fallen asleep. When they woke up, they saw Jesus' glory and the two men standing with him. As Moses and Elijah were starting to leave, Peter, not even knowing what he was saying, blurted out, "Master, it's wonderful for us to be here! Let's make three shelters as memorials—one for you, one for Moses, and one for Elijah." But even as he was saying this, a cloud overshadowed them, and terror gripped them as the cloud covered them. Then a voice from the cloud said, "This is my Son, my Chosen One. Listen to him." When the voice finished, Jesus was there alone. They didn't tell anyone at that time what they had seen.

LUKE 9:28-36

MYSTERY ANSWER:

THE GOOD SAMARITAN

LUKE 10:30-37

See if you can unscramble the mixed-up letters to make the words without looking at the passage first. If you get stumped, look for the answers in the verses below.

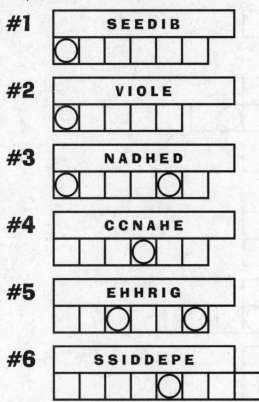

#1 SEEDIB

#2 VIOLE

#3 NADHED

#4 CCNAHE

#5 EHHRIG

#6 SSIDDEPE

Jesus replied with a story: "A Jewish man was traveling from Jerusalem down to Jericho, and he was attacked by bandits. They stripped him of his clothes, beat him up, and left him half dead beside the road. By chance a priest came along. But when he saw the man lying there, he crossed to the other side of the road and passed him by. A Temple assistant walked over and looked at him lying there, but he also passed by on the other side. Then a despised Samaritan came along, and when he saw the man, he felt compassion for him. Going over to him, the Samaritan soothed his wounds with olive oil and wine and bandaged them. Then he put the man on his own donkey and took him to an inn, where he took care of him. The next day he handed the innkeeper two silver coins, telling him, 'Take care of this man. If his bill runs higher than this, I'll pay you the next time I'm here.' Now which of these three would you say was a neighbor to the man who was attacked by bandits?" Jesus asked. The man replied, "The one who showed him mercy." Then Jesus said, "Yes, now go and do the same."

LUKE 10:30-37

MYSTERY ANSWER:

THE LOST SHEEP

LUKE 15:1-7

See if you can unscramble the mixed-up letters to make the words without looking at the passage first. If you get stumped, look for the answers in the verses below.

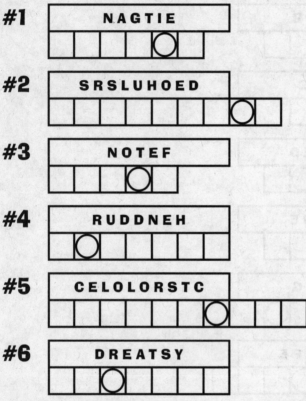

#1 NAGTIE

#2 SRSLUHOED

#3 NOTEF

#4 RUDDNEH

#5 CELOLORSTC

#6 DREATSY

Tax collectors and other notorious sinners often came to listen to Jesus teach. This made the Pharisees and teachers of religious law complain that he was associating with such sinful people— even eating with them! So Jesus told them this story: "If a man has a hundred sheep and one of them gets lost, what will he do? Won't he leave the ninety-nine others in the wilderness and go to search for the one that is lost until he finds it? And when he has found it, he will joyfully carry it home on his shoulders. When he arrives, he will call together his friends and neighbors, saying, 'Rejoice with me because I have found my lost sheep.' In the same way, there is more joy in heaven over one lost sinner who repents and returns to God than over

ninety-nine others who are righteous and haven't strayed away!"

LUKE 15:1-7

MYSTERY ANSWER:

198

AN OFFICIAL'S SON HEALED
JOHN 4:43-54

See if you can unscramble the mixed-up letters to make the words without looking at the passage first. If you get stumped, look for the answers in the verses below.

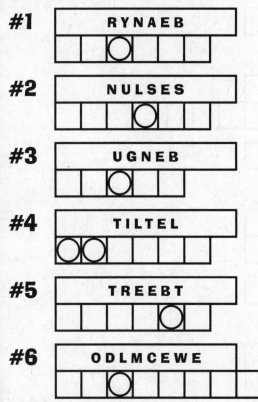

#1 RYNAEB

#2 NULSES

#3 UGNEB

#4 TILTEL

#5 TREEBT

#6 ODLMCEWE

At the end of the two days, Jesus went on to Galilee. He himself had said that a prophet is not honored in his own hometown. Yet the Galileans welcomed him, for they had been in Jerusalem at the Passover celebration and had seen everything he did there. As he traveled through Galilee, he came to Cana, where he had turned the water into wine. There was a government official in nearby Capernaum whose son was very sick. When he heard that Jesus had come from Judea to Galilee, he went and begged Jesus to come to Capernaum to heal his son, who was about to die. Jesus asked, "Will you never believe in me unless you see miraculous signs and wonders?" The official pleaded, "Lord, please come now before my little boy dies." Then Jesus told him, "Go back home. Your son will live!" And the man believed what Jesus said and started home. While the man was on his way, some of his servants met him with the news that his son was alive and well. He asked them when the boy had begun to get better, and they replied, "Yesterday afternoon at one o'clock his fever suddenly disappeared!" Then the father realized that that was the very time Jesus had told him, "Your son will live." And he and his entire household believed in Jesus. This was the second miraculous sign Jesus did in Galilee after coming from Judea.

JOHN 4:43-54

MYSTERY ANSWER:

"GET UP AND WALK"

ACTS 3:1-11

See if you can unscramble the mixed-up letters to make the words without looking at the passage first. If you get stumped, look for the answers in the verses below.

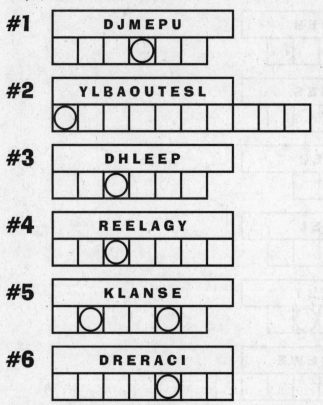

#1 DJMEPU

#2 YLBAOUTESL

#3 DHLEEP

#4 REELAGY

#5 KLANSE

#6 DRERACI

Peter and John went to the Temple one afternoon to take part in the three o'clock prayer service. As they approached the Temple, a man lame from birth was being carried in. Each day he was put beside the Temple gate, the one called the Beautiful Gate, so he could beg from the people going into the Temple. When he saw Peter and John about to enter, he asked them for some money. Peter and John looked at him intently, and Peter said, "Look at us!" The lame man looked at them eagerly, expecting some money. But Peter said, "I don't have any silver or gold for you. But I'll give you what I have. In the name of Jesus Christ the Nazarene, get up and walk!" Then Peter took the lame man by the right hand and helped him up. And as he did, the man's feet and ankles were instantly healed and strengthened. He jumped up, stood on his feet, and began to walk! Then, walking, leaping, and praising God, he went into the Temple with them. All the people saw him walking and heard him praising God. When they realized he was the lame beggar they had seen so often at the Beautiful Gate, they were absolutely astounded! They all rushed out in amazement to Solomon's Colonnade, where the man was holding tightly to Peter and John.

ACTS 3:1-11

MYSTERY ANSWER:

ANSWERS

1. **THE MAN WHO NEVER DIED**
   Jumbles: 1. HEAR | 2. CAIN | 3. BRONZE | 4. FOUNDED |
   5. FELLOWSHIP
   Mystery Answer: ENOCH

2. **TWO BROTHERS MAKE UP**
   Jumbles: 1. ESAU | 2. JACOB | 3. SUCCOTH | 4. EMBRACED |
   5. ACCEPTED
   Mystery Answer: PEACE

3. **A STONE FOR A PILLOW**
   Jumbles: 1. FATHER | 2. GIVING | 3. DREAMED | 4. NUMEROUS |
   5. STAIRWAY
   Mystery Answer: HEAVEN

4. **BROTHER TROUBLE**
   Jumbles: 1. KILL | 2. REUBEN | 3. DREAMER | 4. CISTERN |
   5. DISTANCE
   Mystery Answer: TRICKED

5. **TROUBLE FOR THE EGYPTIANS**
   Jumbles: 1. HAIL | 2. LOCUST | 3. DOWNPOUR | 4. LIVESTOCK |
   5. LIGHTNING
   Mystery Answer: PLAGUE

6. **THE LAST PLAGUE**
   Jumbles: 1. LOUD | 2. OLDEST | 3. BURNING | 4. OFFICIALS |
   5. NEIGHBORS
   Mystery Answer: FIRSTBORN

7. **THE BIG TEN**
   Jumbles: 1. STEAL | 2. FALSELY | 3. SABBATH | 4. TESTIFY |
   5. APPROACH
   Mystery Answer: OBEYS

8. **A HELPER FOR MOSES**
   Jumbles: 1. ROBE | 2. NADAB | 3. SACRED | 4. PRIEST |
   5. GEMSTONE
   Mystery Answer: AARON

9. **FOOD IN THE DESERT**
   Jumbles: 1. MEAT | 2. ANGRY | 3. QUAIL | 4. WHINING |
   5. COMPLAIN
   Mystery Answer: MANNA

10. **A HERO DIES**
    Jumbles: 1. POWER | 2. CLIMBED | 3. SERVANT | 4. ALLOWED |
    5. PROMISED
    Mystery Answer: MOSES

11. **SCOPING OUT THE CITY**
    Jumbles: 1. STRONG | 2. JERICHO | 3. HANGING |
    4. EUPHRATES | 5. COURAGEOUS
    Mystery Answer: SPIES

12. **THE DAY THE SUN AND MOON STAND STILL**
    Jumbles: 1. MIDDLE | 2. FOUGHT | 3. GILGAL | 4. ABANDON |
    5. VICTORY
    Mystery Answer: GIBEON

13. **A SAD STORY WITH A HAPPY ENDING**
    Jumbles: 1. MOAB | 2. OBED | 3. FIELD | 4. FAMINE |
    5. HARVEST
    Mystery Answer: NAOMI

14. **THE ARK IS MISSING!**
    Jumbles: 1. HEAVY | 2. CALVES | 3. PLAGUES | 4. RETURNED |
    5. DESTROYED
    Mystery Answer: CAPTURED

15. **THE NEW KING**
    Jumbles: 1. SAUL | 2. JESSE | 3. MISSION | 4. ANOINTED |
    5. BROTHERS
    Mystery Answer: MODEST

16. **A FURIOUS KING**
    Jumbles: 1. HARP | 2. CYMBALS | 3. JONATHAN |
    4. SUCCESSFUL | 5. TORMENTING
    Mystery Answer: JEALOUSY

17. **A DARING ESCAPE**
    Jumbles: 1. HIDING | 2. SEARCH | 3. RAIDING | 4. REMAINED |
    5. THOUSANDS
    Mystery Answer: DANGEROUS

18. **DAVID REPAYS EVIL WITH GOOD**
    Jumbles: 1. CAVE | 2. HARM | 3. ENEMY | 4. CALLED |
    5. KINGDOM
    Mystery Answer: MERCY

19. **SAUL'S LAST BATTLE**
    Jumbles: 1. OCCUPIED | 2. WARRIORS | 3. ATTACKED |
    4. FIGHTING | 5. SLAUGHTERED
    Mystery Answer: DEFEAT

20. **SOLOMON'S AMAZING BUILDING PROJECT**
    Jumbles: 1. OBEY | 2. HIRAM | 3. JOYFUL | 4. COMMANDS |
    5. CELEBRATION
    Mystery Answer: SANCTUARY

21. A WOMAN WITH WEALTH AND SPLENDOR
Jumbles: 1. SHEBA | 2. JEWELS | 3. CARAVAN | 4. JUSTICE | 5. QUESTIONS
Mystery Answer: QUEEN

22. A KINGDOM SPLITS IN TWO
Jumbles: 1. LABOR | 2. EVENTS | 3. REFUSED | 4. REJECTED | 5. NORTHERN
Mystery Answer: REVOLT

23. THE MAN WHO SAW A CHARIOT OF FIRE
Jumbles: 1. RIVER | 2. HORSES | 3. TALKING | 4. SUDDENLY | 5. WHIRLWIND
Mystery Answer: ELISHA

24. JOASH RESTORES THE HOUSE OF GOD
Jumbles: 1. MONEY | 2. CHEST | 3. WORKMEN | 4. REPAIRED | 5. VOLUNTARY
Mystery Answer: TREASURY

25. A FAITHFUL KING
Jumbles: 1. KING | 2. AHAZ | 3. ROYAL | 4. MESSAGE | 5. CHARIOTS"
Mystery Answer: HEZEKIAH

26. HEZEKIAH SEEKS GOD'S HELP
Jumbles: 1. PLANT | 2. ENTER | 3. DEFEND | 4. LETTER | 5. ASSYRIA
Mystery Answer: PRAYER

27. EXTRA YEARS OF LIFE
Jumbles: 1. SHADOW | 2. FIFTEEN | 3. SERVANT | 4. BACKWARD | 5. OINTMENT
Mystery Answer: RECOVER

28. EVIL IN THE LORD'S SIGHT
Jumbles: 1. PAGAN | 2. ASHERAH | 3. REMNANT | 4. PROPHETS | 5. DETESTABLE
Mystery Answer: MANASSEH

29. HARD WORK, GREAT CELEBRATION
Jumbles: 1. PERSIA | 2. ENDURES | 3. REBUILDING | 4. CARPENTERS | 5. PERMISSION
Mystery Answer: TEMPLE

30. A BIG JOB TO DO
Jumbles: 1. WALLS | 2. DOORS | 3. WORKING | 4. INSPECT | 5. RUBBISH
Mystery Answer: REBUILT

31. A BRAVE AND BEAUTIFUL QUEEN
Jumbles: 1. ADVICE | 2. COUSIN | 3. ESTHER | 4. MAJESTY | 5. BANQUET
Mystery Answer: HEROINE

32. SEND ME!
Jumbles: 1. COAL | 2. GUILT | 3. TRAIN | 4. SERAPHIM | 5. MESSENGER
Mystery Answer: ISAIAH

33. A PROPHET OF DOOM
Jumbles: 1. EXILE | 2. SCATTER | 3. ZEDEKIAH | 4. CAPTIVES | 5. JERUSALEM
Mystery Answer: EZEKIEL

34. GET READY TO GO!
Jumbles: 1. NIGHT | 2. REBELS | 3. BAGGAGE | 4. SHOULDER | 5. DAYLIGHT
Mystery Answer: BABYLON

35. EZEKIEL'S TOUGH JOB
Jumbles: 1. PEACE | 2. SHEEP | 3. ALARM | 4. SAFETY | 5. WARNING
Mystery Answer: WATCHMAN

36. DANIEL'S SPECIAL GIFT
Jumbles: 1. REVEALS | 2. PROSPER | 3. MYSTERY | 4. INTERPRET | 5. DISTURBING
Mystery Answer: DREAMS

37. FROM ABRAHAM TO JESUS
Jumbles: 1. BOAZ | 2. JACOB | 3. TAMAR | 4. SALMON | 5. BATHSHEBA
Mystery Answer: ANCESTORS

38. THE WISE MEN'S QUEST
Jumbles: 1. GOLD | 2. GAVE | 3. MYRRH | 4. GUIDED | 5. CHESTS
Mystery Answer: SAVIOR

39. ESCAPE IN THE NIGHT
Jumbles: 1. MARY | 2. WEEPS | 3. ANGEL | 4. RETURN | 5. JOSEPH
Mystery Answer: EGYPT

40. A STRANGE JOB FOR A FISH
Jumbles: 1. YES | 2. CATCH | 3. TEMPLE | 4. CITIZENS | 5. COLLECTORS
Mystery Answer: PAYMENT

41. JESUS, THE STORYTELLER
Jumbles: 1. LOST | 2. SHEEP | 3. FARMERS | 4. DEBTORS | 5. VINEYARD
Mystery Answer: PARABLE

42. A MIRACLE BY JESUS
Jumbles: 1. WANT | 2. BEGAN | 3. STOPPED | 4. FOLLOWED | 5. DISCIPLES
Mystery Answer: BLINDNESS

43. THREE SERVANTS
Jumbles: 1. SERVANT | 2. USELESS | 3. FAITHFUL | 4. ENTRUSTED | 5. CULTIVATE
Mystery Answer: INVEST

44. A NIGHT OF PRAYER
Jumbles: 1. COME | 2. GRIEF | 3. WATCH | 4. SINNERS | 5. BETRAYED
Mystery Answer: GETHSEMANE

45. PUTTING JESUS ON TRIAL
Jumbles: 1. ROMAN | 2. YELLED | 3. CHARGES | 4. PRIESTS | 5. PRISONER
Mystery Answer: PILATE

46. SOLDIERS MAKE FUN OF JESUS
Jumbles: 1. AWAY | 2. KNELT | 3. CROWN | 4. REGIMENT | 5. BRANCHES
Mystery Answer: MOCKERY

47. THE DARKEST DAY
Jumbles: 1. GUARD | 2. CROSS | 3. CYRENE | 4. SCOFFED | 5. RIDICULED
Mystery Answer: CRUCIFY

48. JESUS AMAZES THE CROWD
Jumbles: 1. QUIET | 2. ORDERS | 3. SABBATH | 4. DESTROY | 5. SHOUTING
Mystery Answer: AUTHORITY

49. MIRACLE FOR A DEAF MAN
Jumbles: 1. SPEECH | 2. BEGGED | 3. PLAINLY | 4. FINGERS | 5. SPITTING
Mystery Answer: HEARING

50. HOW TO BE FIRST IN GOD'S KINGDOM
Jumbles: 1. LAST | 2. HOUSE | 3. LITTLE | 4. CAPERNAUM | 5. DISCUSSING
Mystery Answer: CHILD

51. THE MOST IMPORTANT RULE
Jumbles: 1. LOVE | 2. NEIGHBOR | 3. ANSWERED | 4. STRENGTH | 5. LISTENING
Mystery Answer: LOVING

52. JESUS CELEBRATES PASSOVER
Jumbles: 1. BETRAY | 2. POURED | 3. PIECES | 4. BLESSED | 5. PREPARE
Mystery Answer: SUPPER

53. ZECHARIAH'S BIG MISTAKE
Jumbles: 1. ALTAR | 2. BIRTH | 3. AFRAID | 4. INCENSE | 5. GLADNESS
Mystery Answer: DISBELIEF

54. JOHN THE BAPTIST'S PULPIT
Jumbles: 1. WHEAT | 2. COLLECT | 3. PRODUCE | 4. MESSIAH | 5. WARNINGS
Mystery Answer: WILDERNESS

55. A WOMAN SHOWS HER LOVE
Jumbles: 1. SINS | 2. SAVED | 3. LOANED | 4. PERFUME | 5. KNEELING
Mystery Answer: FORGIVEN

56. JESUS MEETS THE KNOW-IT-ALLS
Jumbles: 1. EXPERT | 2. FILTHY | 3. NEGLECT | 4. WASHING | 5. INSULTED
Mystery Answer: PHARISEES

57. JESUS' SABBATH MIRACLE
Jumbles: 1. LEGS | 2. DINNER | 3. ANSWER | 4. TOUCHED | 5. SWOLLEN
Mystery Answer: HEALING

58. THE ONE WHO SAID THANK YOU
Jumbles: 1. MERCY | 2. GLORY | 3. PRAISE | 4. BORDER | 5. CLEANSED
Mystery Answer: LEPROSY

59. HE IS RISEN!
Jumbles: 1. THIRD | 2. EMPTY | 3. RUSHED | 4. MORNING | 5. CLOTHED
Mystery Answer: RESURRECT

60. NEVER THIRSTY AGAIN
Jumbles: 1. WELL | 2. FRESH | 3. TRUTH | 4. BUCKET | 5. HUSBAND
Mystery Answer: WATER

61. MIRACLE FOR A LAME MAN
Jumbles: 1. SICK | 2. LYING | 3. WATER | 4. BUBBLES | 5. BETHESDA
Mystery Answer: WALKING

62. JESUS SHOWS WHAT HIS FATHER IS LIKE
Jumbles: 1. MOSES | 2. BIRTH | 3. BEGGAR | 4. SILOAM | 5. TRYING
Mystery Answer: GLORY

63. JESUS KNOWS HIS FLOCK
Jumbles: 1. VOICE | 2. SCATTERS | 3. SACRIFICE | 4. SHEEPFOLD | 5. AUTHORITY
Mystery Answer: SHEPHERD

64. JESUS SERVES HIS FRIENDS
Jumbles: 1. BASIN | 2. TOWEL | 3. BELONG | 4. TEACHER | 5. CELEBRATION
Mystery Answer: WASHING

65. ONE GLORIOUS MORNING
Jumbles: 1. EARLY | 2. INSIDE | 3. ROLLED | 4. OUTRAN | 5. DISCIPLE
Mystery Answer: SUNDAY

66. "WHY ARE YOU CRYING?"
Jumbles: 1. PEACE | 2. HANDS | 3. PLACE | 4. FINGER | 5. BELIEVE
Mystery Answer: ALIVE

67. A MIGHTY MOVEMENT OF GOD
Jumbles: 1. CROWD | 2. SPIRIT | 3. ABILITY | 4. EVERYONE | 5. SPEAKING
Mystery Answer: PENTECOST

68. A CHRISTIAN COMMUNITY
Jumbles: 1. HOMES | 2. TEACHING | 3. MIRACULOUS | 4. FELLOWSHIP | 5. GENEROSITY
Mystery Answer: SHARING

69. PETER'S STRANGE EXPERIENCE
Jumbles: 1. STAND | 2. DEVOUT | 3. UNCLEAN | 4. ANIMALS | 5. INVITED
Mystery Answer: VISION

70. A MIRACULOUS ESCAPE
Jumbles: 1. CELL | 2. BRIGHT | 3. SENSES | 4. KNOCKED | 5. WALKING
Mystery Answer: ANGEL

71. THE IMPORTANT MEETING
Jumbles: 1. CHURCH | 2. RESOLVE | 3. PREACHED | 4. FINISHED | 5. CONVERTS
Mystery Answer: COUNCIL

72. PAUL IS CAPTURED
Jumbles: 1. FORCE | 2. MEMBERS | 3. CONFLICT | 4. PHARISEE | 5. ANCESTORS
Mystery Answer: PRISON

73. **PAUL'S IMPORTANT TEACHINGS**
Jumbles: 1. SERVE | 2. FAITH | 3. NOTHING | 4. BELIEVER |
5. TRANSFORM
Mystery Answer: SALVATION

74. **A REQUEST FOR UNITY**
Jumbles: 1. FORCED | 2. HOPING | 3. FELLOW | 4. WELCOME |
5. MENTION
Mystery Answer: PHILEMON

75. **JOHN'S AMAZING VISION**
Jumbles: 1. SEVEN | 2. HEAVEN | 3. WORTHY | 4. TRUMPET |
5. RAINBOW
Mystery Answer: THRONE

MYSTERY PERSON JUMBLES

1. **SOMEONE WITH A LONG LIFE**
Jumbles: 1. HUMAN | 2. LAMECH | 3. DAUGHTERS | 4. YEARS |
5. ENOCH
Mystery Person: METHUSELAH

2. **THE FIRST OF GOD'S CHOSEN PEOPLE**
Jumbles: 1. REWARD | 2. SARAH | 3. STARS | 4. BELIEVED |
5. PROMISED
Mystery Person: ABRAHAM

3. **A DREAMER WHO FINDS ADVENTURE**
Jumbles: 1. JACOB | 2. CAMELS | 3. BROTHERS | 4. PASTURE |
5. STARS
Mystery Person: JOSEPH

4. **A PROPHET WHO SANG**
Jumbles: 1. SISTER | 2. MAID | 3. MOSES | 4. DANCED |
5. PROPHET
Mystery Person: MIRIAM

5. **A STUBBORN RULER**
Jumbles: 1. STAFF | 2. HAIL | 3. RIVER | 4. SERPENT | 5. HORSES
Mystery Person: PHARAOH

6. **A BRAVE YOUNG LEADER**
Jumbles: 1. WARRIORS | 2. AROUND | 3. JERICHO |
4. COLLAPSE | 5. MARCH
Mystery Person: JOSHUA

7. **A FARMER WHO IS CALLED TO FIGHT**
Jumbles: 1. JOASH | 2. FLEECE | 3. VICTORY | 4. JUDGE |
5. MIDNIGHT
Mystery Person: GIDEON

8. **A STRONG MAN IN TROUBLE**
Jumbles: 1. LION | 2. VOWED | 3. HAIR | 4. SWARM | 5. SOREK
Mystery Person: SAMSON

9. **A PRAYING MOTHER**
Jumbles: 1. SHILOH | 2. BASKET | 3. ELKANAH | 4. GRANT |
5. NEEDY
Mystery Person: HANNAH

10. **A GODLY BOY**
Jumbles: 1. SLEEPING | 2. JUDGMENT | 3. RELIABLE |
4. MESSAGES | 5. THREATS
Mystery Person: SAMUEL

11. **AN ENORMOUS ENEMY**
Jumbles: 1. FIVE | 2. FOREHEAD | 3. CONTEMPT | 4. GIANT |
5. STUMBLED
Mystery Person: GOLIATH

12. **THE KING WHO HAD IT ALL**
Jumbles: 1. GOLD | 2. TEMPLE | 3. NATIONS | 4. ROYAL |
5. WISDOM
Mystery Person: SOLOMON

13. **A POWERFUL PROPHET**
Jumbles: 1. RAVENS | 2. WIDOW | 3. ELISHA | 4. JORDAN |
5. CAMPED
Mystery Person: ELIJAH

14. **PROPHET WITH A DOUBLE BLESSING**
Jumbles: 1. RIVER | 2. INHERIT | 3. MASTER | 4. DOUBLE |
5. CLOAK
Mystery Person: ELISHA

15. **A YOUNG KING OF JUDAH**
Jumbles: 1. ZECHARIAH | 2. AMAZIAH | 3. SIXTEEN |
4. BURNED | 5. JOTHAM
Mystery Person: UZZIAH

16. **A GODLY KING**
Jumbles: 1. JUDAH | 2. FATHER | 3. TROOPS | 4. MICAIAH |
5. FORTRESSES
Mystery Person: JEHOSHAPHAT

17. **A WOMAN WHO RESCUED GOD'S PEOPLE**
Jumbles: 1. BANQUET | 2. HAMAN | 3. PURIM | 4. MORDECAI |
5. GLADNESS
Mystery Person: ESTHER

18. **A BRAVE FRIEND**
Jumbles: 1. FLAMES | 2. DETERMINED | 3. SHADRACH |
4. BABYLON | 5. FURNACE
Mystery Person: MESHACH

19. **A NEW TESTAMENT PROPHET**
Jumbles: 1. JESUS | 2. HEAVEN | 3. INSTRUCTIONS | 4. BLIND |
5. PROPHET
Mystery Person: JOHN THE BAPTIST

20. **ONE WHO WASHED HIS HANDS**
Jumbles: 1. PRIESTS | 2. INNOCENT | 3. SURPRISE | 4. RELEASE |
5. FLOGGED
Mystery Person: PILATE

21. **A MAN IN A TREE**
Jumbles: 1. GUEST | 2. TAXES | 3. CHEATED | 4. NAZARENE |
5. SYCAMORE
Mystery Person: ZACCHAEUS

22. **A NIGHTTIME VISITOR**
    Jumbles: 1. EVENING | 2. KINGDOM | 3. TRUTH | 4. SPIRITUAL |
    5. MIRACULOUS
    Mystery Person: NICODEMUS

23. **A BROTHER WHO GETS A SECOND CHANCE**
    Jumbles: 1. SMELL | 2. BETHANY | 3. GRAVE | 4. UNWRAP |
    5. REALIZE
    Mystery Person: LAZARUS

24. **A MAN WHO STRETCHED THE TRUTH**
    Jumbles: 1. LYING | 2. CLAIMING | 3. MONEY | 4. SELLING |
    5. SAPPHIRA
    Mystery Person: ANANIAS

25. **SOMEONE IN THE RIGHT PLACE AT THE RIGHT TIME**
    Jumbles: 1. LOOK | 2. ETHIOPIA | 3. SCRIPTURE | 4. BAPTIZED |
    5. CARRIAGE
    Mystery Person: PHILIP

JUMBLE DETECTIVE

1. **THE CASE OF THE OVERARCHING PROMISE**
   Jumbles: 1. BLESSED | 2. CLOUDS | 3. COVENANT |
   4. CONFIRM | 5. FLOODWATERS
   Mystery Answer: RAINBOW

2. **THE CASE OF THE BROTHERS' BETRAYAL**
   Jumbles: 1. JACOB | 2. DREAMER | 3. POTIPHAR | 4. SCHEME |
   5. REUBEN
   Mystery Answer: JUDAH

3. **THE CASE OF THE BIG ESCAPE**
   Jumbles: 1. KILLED | 2. FOREIGN | 3. GERSHOM |
   4. SHEPHERDS | 5. SLAVERY
   Mystery Answer: MIDIAN

4. **THE CASE OF THE TEN PUNISHMENTS**
   Jumbles: 1. FROGS | 2. CANALS | 3. PREDICTED | 4. SWARMS |
   5. REFUSE
   Mystery Answer: PLAGUES

5. **THE CASE OF THE AMAZING ESCAPE**
   Jumbles: 1. PHARAOH | 2. COUNTRY | 3. PASSOVER |
   4. FIRSTBORN | 5. MIDNIGHT
   Mystery Answer: EGYPT

6. **THE CASE OF THE MIRACULOUS CROSSING**
   Jumbles: 1. SIDES | 2. WHEELS | 3. CLOUD | 4. EGYPTIANS |
   5. CHARIOTEERS
   Mystery Answer: RED SEA

7. **THE CASE OF THE FURIOUS KING**
   Jumbles: 1. JEREMIAH | 2. WEEPING | 3. BRUTAL |
   4. CHILDREN | 5. HEROD
   Mystery Answer: BETHLEHEM

8. **THE CASE OF THE AMAZING MESSAGE**
   Jumbles: 1. BAPTISM | 2. ISAIAH | 3. BRINGS | 4. REQUIRES |
   5. VOICE
   Mystery Answer: HEAVEN

9. **THE CASE OF THE SURPRISED PIGS**
   Jumbles: 1. HERDSMEN | 2. VIOLENT | 3. STEEP | 4. PLUNGED |
   5. CEMETERY
   Mystery Answer: DEMONS

10. **THE CASE OF THE TWELVE-YEAR TROUBLE**
    Jumbles: 1. MOMENT | 2. FAITH | 3. CONSTANT | 4. WELL |
    5. FRINGE
    Mystery Answer: WOMAN

11. **THE CASE OF THE MIGHTY MIRACLES**
    Jumbles: 1. OPPOSES | 2. FEUDING | 3. HEALED | 4. WORLD |
    5. CONDEMN
    Mystery Answer: POWERFUL

12. **THE CASE OF PETER'S AMAZING REVELATION**
    Jumbles: 1. FORBID | 2. GIVE | 3. KEYS | 4. SIMON | 5. HEAVEN
    Mystery Answer: KINGDOM

13. **THE CASE OF THE TRAITOROUS FRIEND**
    Jumbles: 1. TRAITOR | 2. CLUBS | 3. GRABBED | 4. JESUS |
    5. SWORDS
    Mystery Answer: JUDAS

14. **THE CASE OF THE DESTROYED DRAPE**
    Jumbles: 1. SANCTUARY | 2. TOMBS | 3. EARTHQUAKE |
    4. TRULY | 5. SPLIT
    Mystery Answer: CURTAIN

15. **THE CASE OF THE SICK MOTHER-IN-LAW**
    Jumbles: 1. ANDREW | 2. AFTER | 3. VARIOUS | 4. HELPED |
    5. DEMONS
    Mystery Answer: FEVER

16. **THE CASE OF JESUS' TRUE IDENTITY**
    Jumbles: 1. ELIJAH | 2. SPITTING | 3. HOME | 4. EYES |
    5. TOUCH
    Mystery Answer: MESSIAH

17. **THE CASE OF THE FORCEFUL FAITH**
    Jumbles: 1. GROUND | 2. FAITHLESS | 3. VIOLENTLY |
    4. MOUTH | 5. INSTANTLY
    Mystery Answer: ANYTHING

18. **THE CASE OF THE MISSING BOY**
    Jumbles: 1. FESTIVAL | 2. TWELVE | 3. TRAVELERS | 4. JESUS |
    5. AMAZED
    Mystery Answer: JERUSALEM

19. **THE CASE OF THE WEEPING WIDOW**
Jumbles: 1. COFFIN | 2. MOTHER | 3. YOUNG | 4. VILLAGE |
5. BEARERS
Mystery Answer: FUNERAL

20. **THE CASE OF BREAD FROM HEAVEN**
Jumbles: 1. THIRSTY | 2. GIVE | 3. MANNA | 4. MIRACULOUS |
5. TRUE
Mystery Answer: HUNGRY

21. **THE CASE OF THE DISBELIEVING DISCIPLE**
Jumbles: 1. WOUNDS | 2. DOORS | 3. EXCLAIMED | 4. TWELVE |
5. FAITHLESS
Mystery Answer: THOMAS

22. **THE CASE OF THE VERY LONG NIGHT**
Jumbles: 1. SHORE | 2. BREAKFAST | 3. GLORIFY | 4. TUNIC |
5. NATHANAEL
Mystery Answer: FISHING

23. **THE CASE OF THE DRAMATIC ROAD TRIP**
Jumbles: 1. SCALES | 2. STRAIGHT | 3. CHOSEN |
4. PERSECUTING | 5. DOWN
Mystery Answer: RENEWED

24. **THE CASE OF THE NEW MISSIONARY PARTNER**
Jumbles: 1. ANTIOCH | 2. CITIZENS | 3. CYPRUS | 4. SAILED |
5. JOINED
Mystery Answer: SILAS

25. **THE CASE OF THE PREACHING PARTNER**
Jumbles: 1. EPHESUS | 2. INSTRUCTIONS | 3. WORSHIP |
4. APOSTLE | 5. MERCY
Mystery Answer: TIMOTHY

JUMBLE CRISS-CROSS

1. **GOD MAKES THE WORLD**
Jumbles: 2A. GATORS | 6A. EARTH | 7A. SWANS | 1D. GARDEN |
3D. TORCH | 4D. LIFE | 5D. BIRDS
Mystery Answer: CREATION

2. **TWO EVIL CITIES**
Jumbles: 3A. JOKING | 4A. LOGICAL | 7A. EAGER |
1D. VILLAGE | 2D. COLUMN | 5D. CREEP | 6D. HURRY
Mystery Answer: GOMORRAH

3. **EXTREME OBEDIENCE**
Jumbles: 1A. KNIFE | 5A. CAUGHT | 7A. CHILD | 8A. FARTHER |
2D. ISAAC | 3D. ENGLISH | 4D. VOTED | 6D. CLIFF
Mystery Answer: SACRIFICE

4. **A STRUGGLE WITH GOD**
Jumbles: 1A. WIVES | 4A. INJURY | 5A. LANE | 6A. WOKE |
7A. MATCH | 2D. IGNORE | 3D. SERVANT
Mystery Answer: WRESTLE

5. **THE BUSH THAT DIDN'T BURN UP**
Jumbles: 1A. FRIGHTEN | 3A. BIBLE | 5A. GROUND |
6A. RECORDED | 1D. FIRE | 2D. EVENING | 4D. SOUND
Mystery Answer: ENGULFED

6. **A YEARLY CELEBRATION**
Jumbles: 1A. FIRST | 2A. LAMB | 6A. HOMES | 7A. ENJOYS |
1D. FEAST | 3D. BLOODY | 4D. LIVES | 5D. PRIDE
Mystery Answer: PASSOVER

7. **THE ISRAELITES DISOBEY**
Jumbles: 2A. CALF | 5A. EARRING | 6A. MOLDED | 1D. OFFER |
3D. ANGER | 4D. TURNED
Mystery Answer: GOLDEN

8. **A TALKING ANIMAL**
Jumbles: 1A. COAST | 4A. CURSE | 6A. ANNOY | 2D. SPEAK |
3D. SWORD | 5D. UNTIE
Mystery Answer: DONKEY

9. **AS CLOSE AS BROTHERS**
Jumbles: 3A. THERE | 4A. STEERING | 6A. JOKES | 1D. FRIENDS |
2D. HIDING | 4D. SPEAR | 5D. GATES
Mystery Answer: JONATHAN

10. **SEVEN DIPS IN THE RIVER**
Jumbles: 3A. MASTER | 4A. COMPARES | 1D. SEVEN |
2D. ACCEPT | 5D. MULES | 6D. AGAIN
Mystery Answer: NAAMAN

11. **SADNESS OVER A CITY**
Jumbles: 1A. SHAME | 6A. SICKNESS | 7A. HONOR |
2D. HEIGHT | 3D. MAKING | 4D. FISTS | 5D. FEAR
Mystery Answer: NEHEMIAH

12. **A PROPHET WITH A TOUGH JOB**
Jumbles: 1A. PUNISH | 5A. WAILS | 6A. RESTORE | 7A. GOOFY |
2D. NOISES | 3D. SOMEBODY | 4D. POTTER
Mystery Answer: WEEPING

13. **A NIGHT WITH THE LIONS**
Jumbles: 1A. HEROINES | 4A. DARIUS | 5A. PRAYED |
1D. HANDLE | 2D. OFFICER | 3D. NURSERY
Mystery Answer: DANIEL

14. **A VISION IN THE NIGHT**
Jumbles: 1A. DAVID | 4A. PUBLIC | 6A. COMPLETE |
7A. HAPPEN | 2D. VOLUME | 3D. NEWEST | 5D. SECRET
Mystery Answer: APPEARED

15. **HEALING ON THE LORD'S DAY**
Jumbles: 2A. BOAST | 5A. HAND | 6A. OPERATED | 1D. SIGHT |
2D. BRING | 3D. SUBJECTS | 4D. HEARD
Mystery Answer: SABBATH

16. **JESUS ON TRIAL**
Jumbles: 2A. PRISONER | 4A. LEAVE | 5A. NAPKIN | 1D. DEATH |
2D. PALACE | 3D. IMAGINE
Mystery Answer: RELEASE

17. JESUS' FINAL INSTRUCTIONS
Jumbles: 1A. PRICE | 5A. ELEVEN | 7A. AFRICAN | 8A. SAFEST | 2D. CLOVER | 3D. COMMAND | 4D. ALWAYS | 6D. NECKS
Mystery Answer: DISCIPLES

18. THROUGH THE ROOF
Jumbles: 1A. CARRY | 5A. HOLE | 7A. TIDAL | 8A. RAPIDLY | 2D. ROOFTOP | 3D. YIELD | 4D. FINALLY | 6D. TEARS
Mystery Answer: PARALYTIC

19. BACK TO LIFE!
Jumbles: 1A. PIRATE | 5A. ORDER | 6A. ORANGE | 7A. THOROUGH | 1D. PROPHET | 2D. RADIO | 3D. TORNADO | 4D. LUGGAGE
Mystery Answer: DAUGHTER

20. AN INCREDIBLE ANNOUNCEMENT
Jumbles: 1A. THINK | 4A. POWER | 5A. ANGEL | 1D. TERROR | 2D. NEWBORN | 3D. APRIL
Mystery Answer: GABRIEL

21. TWO SISTERS HAVE COMPANY
Jumbles: 1A. DETAILS | 4A. GLIMPSE | 5A. THING | 1D. DAGGER | 2D. THIRST | 3D. LISTEN
Mystery Answer: MARTHA

22. GOD SEES THE HEART
Jumbles: 1A. NIGHT | 4A. MANY | 6A. PRAYER | 7A. SORROW | 2D. HUMBLE | 3D. TEMPLE | 5D. THANKS
Mystery Answer: PHARISEE

23. FAREWELL . . . FOR NOW
Jumbles: 1A. TOUCH | 3A. APPEAR | 6A. HONEST | 7A. STARTLE | 2D. URGENT | 4D. RISE | 5D. CHASE
Mystery Answer: ASCENSION

24. FAITHFUL TO THE END
Jumbles: 1A. MARTYR | 4A. ROCKS | 7A. RETIRING | 2D. ARREST | 3D. RESPONSE | 5D. CHARGE | 6D. DARES
Mystery Answer: STEPHEN

25. MONEY CAN'T BUY GOD'S POWER
Jumbles: 1A. SHARE | 5A. PURCHASE | 6A. EXCITING | 7A. AMONG | 1D. SIMPLE | 2D. REACTION | 3D. STRENGTH | 4D. MAGIC
Mystery Answer: SORCERER

FIND THE JUMBLES

1. DISASTER AND DELIVERANCE
Jumbles: 1. FLOOD | 2. FORTY | 3. COVERING | 4. SCURRY | 5. DESTROY

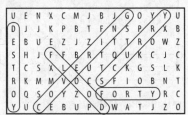

2. TWO BROTHERS MAKE PEACE
Jumbles: 1. TREAT | 2. GIFTS | 3. FAMILY | 4. ESAU | 5. BROTHER

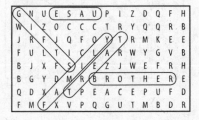

3. PHARAOH'S NIGHTMARES
Jumbles: 1. GRASS | 2. GRAIN | 3. MAGICIANS | 4. FAMINE | 5. PROSPERITY

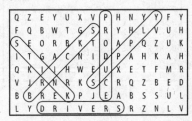

4. TOUGH TIMES IN EGYPT
Jumbles: 1. SUPPLY | 2. BRICKS | 3. DRIVERS | 4. PRODUCE | 5. STINK

5. RAHAB TO THE RESCUE
Jumbles: 1. SPIES | 2. COME | 3. HIDDEN | 4. SCOUT | 5. WINDOW

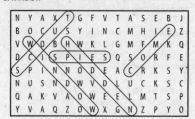

6. TRUSTING GOD IN TOUGH TIMES
Jumbles: 1. STRUGGLE | 2. MISERY | 3. REPENT | 4. JUSTICE | 5. INNOCENCE

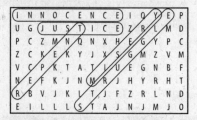

7. GOD KNOWS YOU, INSIDE AND OUT
Jumbles: 1. HEART | 2. PRESENCE | 3. FOLLOW | 4. EXAMINED | 5. THOUGHTS

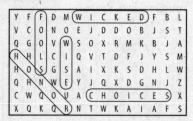

8. WORDS OF WISDOM
Jumbles: 1. FOOLS | 2. HONOR | 3. WICKED | 4. WISE | 5. CHOICES

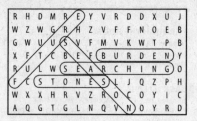

9. A TIME FOR EVERYTHING
Jumbles: 1. SEARCHING | 2. BURDEN | 3. SEASON | 4. FUTURE | 5. STONES

10. THE WRITING ON THE WALL
Jumbles: 1. HAND | 2. NOBLES | 3. PALE | 4. HUMBLED | 5. PURPLE

11. A FAMOUS SERMON
Jumbles: 1. TEMPT | 2. FORGIVE | 3. HEAVEN | 4. BREAD | 5. HOLY

12. WALKING ON WATER
Jumbles: 1. GHOST | 2. ROWING | 3. TOWARD | 4. SERIOUS | 5. COURAGE

13. LITTLE BECOMES MUCH
Jumbles: 1. BOAT | 2. ENOUGH | 3. WANTED | 4. PICKED | 5. BROKE

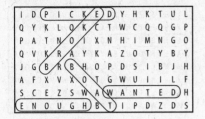

14. CLEARING THE TEMPLE
Jumbles: 1. DOVES | 2. THIEVES | 3. BUYING | 4. TURNED | 5. HOUSE

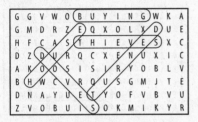

15. JESUS IS PUT IN THE GRAVE
Jumbles: 1. FRIDAY | 2. JOSEPH | 3. LINEN | 4. STONE | 5. ENTRANCE

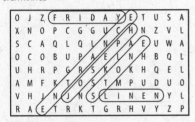

16. THE BEST NEWS
Jumbles: 1. LOOKING | 2. TOMB | 3. EVENING | 4. BURIAL | 5. ENTERED

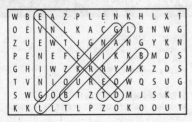

17. GOOD NEWS OF GREAT JOY
Jumbles: 1. SAVIOR | 2. WRAPPED | 3. GLORY | 4. FIELDS | 5. FLOCKS

18. LOST AND FOUND
Jumbles: 1. COIN | 2. SINNER | 3. DIVIDE | 4. REJOICE | 5. SWEEP

19. MIRACLE AT A WEDDING
Jumbles: 1. WINE | 2. DRINK | 3. WEDDING | 4. SERVANTS | 5. GALLONS

20. THE LIGHT GOD SENT TO EARTH
Jumbles: 1. LIGHT | 2. FATHER | 3. COME | 4. DARKNESS | 5. JUDGMENT

21. SHIPWRECK!

Jumbles: 1. STORM | 2. AFRAID | 3. DAWNING | 4. SAILORS | 5. CARGO

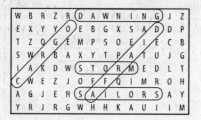

22. WHAT LOVE LOOKS LIKE

Jumbles: 1. PATIENT | 2. GIVES | 3. FOREVER | 4. ENDURES | 5. GAINED

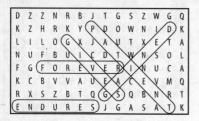

23. GOD'S ARMOR

Jumbles: 1. ENEMY | 2. ARMOR | 3. SHIELD | 4. HELMET | 5. ARROWS

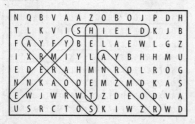

24. THE KIND OF FAITH THAT PLEASES GOD

Jumbles: 1. TONGUE | 2. ENDURE | 3. POISON | 4. WISDOM | 5. CHANGES

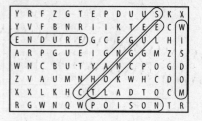

25. A VISION OF HEAVEN

Jumbles: 1. CHURCHES | 2. CITIES | 3. SOULS | 4. SEIZED | 5. DRAGON

BIBLE PASSAGE JUMBLES

1. THE CALL OF ABRAM
Jumbles: 1. BLESSING | 2. ANOTHER | 3. ALTAR | 4. LAND | 5. NATIVE | 6. INSTRUCTED
Mystery Answer: NATION

2. THE BIRTH OF ISAAC
Jumbles: 1. DECLARED | 2. EIGHT | 3. NURSE | 4. EXACTLY | 5. BORN | 6. BECAME
Mystery Answer: LAUGHTER

3. THE SCOUTING REPORT
Jumbles: 1. STOOD | 2. DEVOUR | 3. BEFORE | 4. COUNTRY | 5. LIVING | 6. AGAINST
Mystery Answer: BOUNTIFUL

4. JONAH'S PRAYER
Jumbles: 1. THREW | 2. BACKS | 3. MERCIES | 4. DEPTHS | 5. MIGHTY | 6. DRIVEN
Mystery Answer: PRAISE

5. JESUS' TEMPTATION
Jumbles: 1. HIGH | 2. SHOWED | 3. DURING | 4. PEAK | 5. ALONE | 6. STONE
Mystery Answer: WILDERNESS

6. SERMON ON THE MOUNT
Jumbles: 1. THEIRS | 2. GLAD | 3. BLESSES | 4. HUMBLE | 5. ABOUT | 6. REALIZE
Mystery Answer: BEATITUDES

7. COUNTING THE COST
Jumbles: 1. RELIGIOUS | 2. FOXES | 3. PLACE | 4. LORD | 5. WHEREVER | 6. AROUND
Mystery Answer: DISCIPLES

8. JESUS CALMS THE STORM
Jumbles: 1. DROWN | 2. BREAKING | 3. WINDS | 4. SUDDENLY | 5. OBEY
Mystery Answer: REBUKED

9. **JESUS HEALS THE BLIND**
   Jumbles: 1. MAKE | 2. FAME | 3. BLIND | 4. HAPPEN | 5. DAVID | 6. BEHIND
   Mystery Answer: BELIEVE

10. **JESUS VS. A DEMON**
    Jumbles: 1. DEMON | 2. BROUGHT | 3. BECAUSE | 4. NOTHING | 5. EXCLAIMED | 6. POSSESSED
    Mystery Answer: CAST OUT

11. **JESUS ENTERS JERUSALEM**
    Jumbles: 1. MOUNT | 2. PROCESSION | 3. UPROAR | 4. DISCIPLES | 5. DONKEY | 6. BETHPHAGE
    Mystery Answer: PROPHECY

12. **JESUS IN GETHSEMANE**
    Jumbles: 1. GROVE | 2. GRIEF | 3. FARTHER | 4. JAMES | 5. CRUSHED | 6. SONS
    Mystery Answer: SUFFERING

13. **PETER DENIES JESUS**
    Jumbles: 1. CROWS | 2. OATH | 3. BITTERLY | 4. FLASHED | 5. FRONT | 6. NAZARETH
    Mystery Answer: ROOSTER

14. **JOHN'S BIRTH**
    Jumbles: 1. VERY | 2. WRITING | 3. SURELY | 4. REFLECTED | 5. ASKED | 6. HAPPENED
    Mystery Answer: SPECIAL

15. **THE BIRTH OF JESUS**
    Jumbles: 1. AVAILABLE | 2. OBVIOUSLY | 3. REGISTER | 4. SNUGLY | 5. CLOTH | 6. HOME
    Mystery Answer: BETHLEHEM

16. **JESUS IN THE TEMPLE**
    Jumbles: 1. BABY | 2. GIVEN | 3. THEN | 4. OFFERED | 5. REQUIRED | 6. CONCEIVED
    Mystery Answer: DEDICATED

17. **THE FIRST DISCIPLES**
    Jumbles: 1. FULL | 2. PUSH | 3. SINNER | 4. PARTNERS | 5. NUMBER | 6. AWESTRUCK
    Mystery Answer: FISHERMEN

18. **JESUS CURES LEPROSY**
    Jumbles: 1. ANYONE | 2. REACHED | 3. DESPITE | 4. EXAMINE | 5. ALONG | 6. WITHDREW
    Mystery Answer: CLEANSED

19. **A ROMAN OFFICER'S FAITH**
    Jumbles: 1. BUILT | 2. SAYING | 3. WORTHY | 4. DESERVES | 5. HIGHLY | 6. VALUED
    Mystery Answer: AUTHORITY

20. **JESUS FEEDS A CROWD**
    Jumbles: 1. FEED | 2. LOAVES | 3. WANTED | 4. LOOKED | 5. SLIPPED | 6. FARMS
    Mystery Answer: LEFTOVERS

21. **GOD REVEALED**
    Jumbles: 1. DAZZLING | 2. FALLEN | 3. PRAYING | 4. CLOTHES | 5. GRIPPED | 6. BLURTED
    Mystery Answer: TRANSFIGURED

22. **THE GOOD SAMARITAN**
    Jumbles: 1. BESIDE | 2. OLIVE | 3. HANDED | 4. CHANCE | 5. HIGHER | 6. DESPISED
    Mystery Answer: NEIGHBOR

23. **THE LOST SHEEP**
    Jumbles: 1. EATING | 2. SHOULDERS | 3. OFTEN | 4. HUNDRED | 5. COLLECTORS | 6. STRAYED
    Mystery Answer: RETURN

24. **AN OFFICIAL'S SON HEALED**
    Jumbles: 1. NEARBY | 2. UNLESS | 3. BEGUN | 4. LITTLE | 5. BETTER | 6. WELCOMED
    Mystery Answer: GALILEE

25. **"GET UP AND WALK"**
    Jumbles: 1. JUMPED | 2. ABSOLUTELY | 3. HELPED | 4. EAGERLY | 5. ANKLES | 6. CARRIED
    Mystery Answer: LEAPING